MOSES

GOD'S MAN FOR A CRISIS

BIBLE STUDY GUIDE

From the Bible-teaching ministry of

Charles R. Swindoll

Published by

INSIGHT FOR LIVING

Post Office Box 4444
Fullerton, California 92634

Distributed by

WORD

Educational Products Division
Waco, Texas 76796

These studies are based on the outlines of sermons delivered by Charles R. Swindoll. Chuck is a graduate of Dallas Theological Seminary and has served in pastorates for over twenty-two years, including churches in Texas, New England, and California. Since 1971 he has served as senior pastor of the First Evangelical Free Church of Fullerton, California. Chuck's radio program, "Insight for Living," began in 1979. In addition to his church and radio ministries, Chuck has authored twenty books and numerous booklets on a variety of subjects.

Chuck's outlines are expanded from the sermon transcripts and edited by Bill Watkins, a graduate of California State University at Fresno and Dallas Theological Seminary, with the assistance of Bill Butterworth, a graduate of Florida Bible College, Dallas Theological Seminary, and Florida Atlantic University. Bill Watkins is presently the director of educational resources, and Bill Butterworth is currently the director of counseling ministries at Insight for Living.

Publisher:	Insight for Living, Fullerton, California
Creative Director:	Cynthia Swindoll
Editor:	Bill Watkins
Associate Editor:	Bill Butterworth
Editorial Assistants:	Rebecca Anderson, Nancy Cloud, Debbie Gibbs, Jane Gillis, Wendy Jones, Julie Martin, and Karene Wells
Communications Manager:	Carla Beck
Communications Coordinator:	Alene Cooper
Production Supervisor:	Deedee Snyder
Production Assistant:	Linda Robertson
Production Artists:	Trina Crockett, Ed Kesterson, and Donna Mayo
Typographer:	Trina Crockett
Calligrapher:	Richard Stumpf
Cover Designer:	Michael Standlee
Printer:	R. R. Donnelley & Sons Co.
Cover:	Cover photograph by Dewitt Jones

An album that contains twenty messages on ten cassettes and corresponds to this study guide may be purchased through Insight for Living, Post Office Box 4444, Fullerton, California 92634. For information, please write for the current Insight for Living catalog, or call (714) 870-9161. Canadian residents may direct their correspondence to Insight for Living Ministries, Post Office Box 2510, Vancouver, British Columbia, Canada V6B 3W7, or call (604) 669-1916.

Unless otherwise identified, all Scripture references are from the New American Standard Bible, © The Lockman Foundation 1960, 1962, 1963, 1968, 1971, 1972, 1973, 1975, 1977. Used by permission.

ISBN 0-8499-8217-0

Table of Contents

Moses
God's Man for a Crisis

Moses . . . just the reading of that name sends our minds spinning into orbit!

He was born after midnight in the history of the Hebrews . . . found by Pharaoh's daughter in the Nile . . . nurtured at his mother's breast for only a few precious years before being deposited into the secularized lifestyle of an Egyptian culture. Broken and confused at his mid-life crisis, the man fled to the desert with murder on his record—fully convinced he was a washout. He married, watched his father-in-law's flock, and endured forty years of obscurity, solitude, and silence as God remade and readied him for the epochal moment of his life—the Exodus.

You and I will have little difficulty identifying with the man's frustrations and failures. Nor will we struggle trying to understand the pain of being "shelved" for an extended period of time. But we shall be thrilled to hear again that our God is still in the business of using broken and scarred vessels, bruised with adversity, to accomplish His plan.

Moses . . . he, being dead, still speaks! As you study with us, be sensitive to God's voice. It is loud and clear.

Chuck Swindoll

Putting Truth into Action

Knowledge apart from application falls short of God's desire for His children. Knowledge must result in change and growth. Consequently, we have constructed this Bible study guide with these purposes in mind: (1) to stimulate discovery, (2) to increase understanding, and (3) to encourage application.

At the end of each lesson is a section called *Living Insights.* There you'll be given assistance in further Bible study, thoughtful interaction, and personal appropriation. This is the place where the lesson is fitted with shoe leather for your walk through the varied experiences of life.

In wrapping up some lessons, you'll find a unit called **Digging Deeper.** It will provide you with essential information and list helpful resource materials so that you can probe further into some of the issues raised in those studies.

It's our hope that you'll discover numerous ways to use this tool. Some useful avenues we would suggest are personal meditation, joint discovery, and discussion with your spouse, family, work associates, friends, or neighbors. The study guide is also practical for church classes, and, of course, as a study aid for the "Insight for Living" radio broadcast. The individual studies can usually be completed in thirty minutes. However, some are more open-ended and could be expanded for greater depth. Their use is flexible!

In order to derive the greatest benefit from this process, we suggest that you record your responses to the lessons in a notebook where writing space is plentiful. In view of the kinds of questions asked, your notebook may become a journal filled with your many discoveries and commitments. We anticipate you will find yourself returning to it periodically for review and encouragement.

Bill Watkins
Editor

Bill Butterworth
Associate Editor

MOSES

GOD'S MAN FOR A CRISIS

Misery, Midwives, and Murder
Exodus 1

"God helps those who help themselves" is a common saying tossed around today. This proverb is contradicted throughout Scripture, but perhaps it is opposed no more clearly than in the life of Moses. Through this Old Testament figure, we will discover that *God helps those who trust in Him.* Indeed, He will often place individuals in positions where they must depend on Him alone in order to survive and succeed. Moses was one of these persons; he was God's man for a crisis. As we step into his sandals and walk down the paths he trod, let's take the time to drink from the wells of divine guidance that are provided along the way. For in them, we will find the refreshment and nourishment we need for continuing our journey through the valleys and over the mountains of life.

I. Some Essential Background.
In order to understand why a person thinks and acts the way he does, we must get a handle on his times. And we cannot fully appreciate his era unless we gain some data about the crucial events that shaped it. So let's step back into history and begin our travels four hundred years prior to the birth of Moses. In passing through these centuries on our return trip to Moses' day, we will learn a great deal about the Hebrew people. We will discover how they got to Egypt and why they so desperately needed God to bring them out.

    A. Arrival in Egypt. Around the nineteenth century B.C., a child named Joseph was born into the family of Jacob.* Because he was loved so greatly by Jacob, he was intensely hated by his brothers (Gen. 37:3–4). So they sold him to a group of traders, who in turn took him to Egypt and sold him to "Potiphar, Pharaoh's officer, the captain of the bodyguard" (Gen. 37:18–36). Joseph was misunderstood and mistreated for a period of time, but then the Lord saw fit to elevate him to a place of high honor in the Egyptian government. As Egypt's prime minister, he ruled

---

*The reasons for adopting a nineteenth century B.C. date for Joseph are provided by the Old Testament scholar Gleason Archer in his book *A Survey of Old Testament Introduction,* rev. ed. (Chicago: Moody Press, 1974), pp. 215–19.

over the whole land with only Pharaoh as his superior (Gen. 41:38–44). During the first seven years of his reign, he executed a storage plan that prepared Egypt for a great famine that would devastate the country (Gen. 41:28–32, 46–49). Once the famine began, "the people of all the earth came to Egypt to buy grain from Joseph, because the famine was severe in all the earth" (v. 57). It was this catastrophe that eventually reunited Joseph with his father and brothers. Pharaoh granted Jacob's family permission to settle in the "land of Goshen," the finest piece of real estate in Egypt (Gen. 47:5–6). Jacob accepted Pharaoh's generous offer and moved his family from Canaan to Egypt (Gen. 47:11–12).

B. Prosperity in Egypt. As time passed, Jacob's family acquired more property in Goshen and became economically prosperous. They also began to multiply in population as the sons married and had children (Gen. 47:27). This financial and familial growth continued unhindered for quite a while. When Moses finally arrived on the scene, the Hebrews were greater in number and power than the Egyptians living around them (Exod. 1:7, 9).

C. Brutality in Egypt. Approximately 350 years after Joseph's death, a new Pharaoh reigned in Egypt who knew nothing about Joseph and his service in the Egyptian government (Exod. 1:8). This king was fearful that the Hebrews would turn against the Egyptians in the event of war and " 'depart from the land' " (v. 10), leaving Egypt defeated and destitute. Furthermore, the Egyptians loathed the Hebrews because they practiced shepherding (Gen. 46:31–34)—an occupation that was viewed in the agrarian Egyptian culture as barbaric. As a result of these factors, the new ruler over Egypt instituted an oppressive policy with regard to the Hebrews. And as the Hebrews increased in number, so did the intensity of the Egyptians' brutality. Let's read how the biblical text describes it.

> So they [the Egyptians] appointed taskmasters over them [the Hebrews] to afflict them with hard labor. And they built for Pharaoh storage cities, Pithom and Raamses. But the more they afflicted them, the more they multiplied and the more they spread out, so that they were in dread of the sons of Israel. And the Egyptians compelled the sons of Israel to labor rigorously; and they made their lives bitter with hard labor in mortar and bricks and at all kinds of labor in the field, all their labors which they rigorously imposed on them. (Exod. 1:11–14)

As if this was not enough, Pharaoh instructed the two leading midwives of the Hebrews to murder all the newborn Hebrew males (vv. 15–16). Apparently, they were to suffocate the male babies so that it appeared the children were stillborn. But the midwives refused to obey the king's command because they "feared God" (v. 17). And when Pharaoh asked them why they were allowing the Hebrew sons to live, the midwives lied, saying, " 'Because the Hebrew women are not as the Egyptian women; for they are vigorous, and they give birth before the midwife can get to them' " (vv. 18–19). In spite of their deceit, God blessed the midwives for preserving innocent human beings out of reverence for Him (vv. 20–21). But this did not stop Pharaoh. When he saw that Hebrew males were not being killed at birth, he "commanded all his people, saying, 'Every [Hebrew] son who is born you are to cast into the Nile, and every daughter you are to keep alive' " (v. 22).

D. God's Promise to the Hebrews. Although a beautiful picture of prosperity had turned to an ugly scene of brutality, the Hebrew people had a divine promise to cling to. The Lord gave it to Abraham in these words:

"Know for certain that your descendants will be strangers in a land that is not theirs, where they will be enslaved and oppressed four hundred years. But I will also judge the nation whom they will serve; and afterward they will come out with many possessions." (Gen. 15:13–14)

Their trial would be long and harsh, but it would not be permanent. God told them that He would provide an exodus. And, as we shall see, the Lord fulfilled His promise through a Hebrew shepherd named Moses.

II. Some Timeless Lessons.

Even though these events occurred about four thousand years ago, they communicate principles for life that transcend the barriers of history. Among these lessons, three are especially important.

A. Hard times don't erase God's promises. If the sovereign King says that He will accomplish something, then He will do it regardless of how bleak the situation may seem. We can count on it!

B. Harsh treatment doesn't escape God's notice. The omniscient Lord not only knew that His people were suffering in Egypt (cf. Exod. 3:7), but He had prophesied centuries before that they would become objects of the Egyptians' hatred (Gen. 15:13). As the Book of Hebrews says, "All things are open and laid bare to the eyes of Him with whom we have to do" (Heb. 4:13b). Since nothing escapes His notice, believers can rest assured that He is aware of any ill-treatment they might be experiencing.

C. Heavy tests don't eclipse God's concern. Like the Hebrews, we may go through difficult periods in our lives. We might even be commanded by superiors to commit wrongful acts, as were the Hebrew midwives. However, we can be confident in the fact that God will one day reward us for our obedience and deliver us from our temporary tribulations.

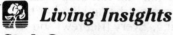 *Living Insights*

Study One ▬▬▬▬▬▬▬▬▬▬▬▬▬▬▬▬▬▬▬▬▬▬▬▬▬▬▬▬▬▬▬▬▬▬▬

Moses: God's Man for a Crisis—the title of our study guide rings with relevance. Let's take a few minutes to get better acquainted with the man who will be our focus in the following lessons.

• Copy this chart into your notebook. Then look at the lesson titles and Scripture references that have been listed. As you read the passages given, record your observations, questions, and comments. Don't be frustrated if you have a lot of questions. Hopefully our studies will provide you with the necessary tools for discovering the answers. This overview will grant you a foretaste of good things to come.

Moses: God's Man for a Crisis	
Titles and Texts	Observations, Questions, and Comments
Misery, Midwives, and Murder *Exodus 1*	
Born After Midnight *Exodus 2:1–10*	
God's Will, My Way *Exodus 2:10–15, Acts 7:21–29*	
Lessons Learned from Failure *Exodus 2:11–25, Psalm 119:67,71*	
The Desert: School of Self-discovery *Exodus 2:21–22,3:1; Acts 7:29–30a*	
Burning Bridges or Burning Bushes *Exodus 3:1–10*	
Who Me, Lord? *Exodus 3:10–4:19*	

Continued on next page

4

Moses: God's Man for a Crisis—Continued

Titles and Texts	Observations, Questions, and Comments
God's Will, God's Way *Exodus 4:18–31*	
Going from Bad to Worse *Exodus 5–6*	
Plagues That Preach *Exodus 7–10*	
The Night Nobody Slept *Exodus 11–12*	
Between the Devil and the Deep Red Sea *Exodus 14*	
A Heavenly Diet vs. an Earthly Appetite *Exodus 15:1–17:7*	
Why Leaders Crack Up *Exodus 18*	
Sinai: Where Moses Met God *Exodus 19–31*	
Particular Perils of the Godly *Numbers 10–14*	
A Moment of Rage *Numbers 20:1–13*	
Filling the Shoes of Moses *Numbers 27:12–23*	
Obituary of a Hero *Deuteronomy 34*	
Moses' Faith, Moses' Choices . . . and Me Hebrews 11:24–28	

Living Insights

Study Two

Can you relate to hard times, harsh treatment, and/or heavy tests? Then this series is going to be very appropriate. Use the italicized words in the questions below as headings for your thoughts. These queries will help you take inventory of the struggles you currently face. Don't forget the last question. It is key!

- What are the *hard times* in my life right now?
- What is the *harsh treatment* I am currently facing?
- What *heavy tests* am I presently enduring?
- Where is *God* in all of this?

5

⚒ Digging Deeper

The lie told by the midwives in order to save the Hebrew male newborns illustrates a reoccurring moral dilemma. The problem is this: When moral laws come into conflict, which one is a believer obligated to obey and why? In the case of the Hebrew midwives, the conflicting absolute norms were obeying the government, telling the truth, and saving innocent lives. As we discovered, they kept the third law but broke the other two. Was their action right or wrong? This question has been answered three different ways by Christians. Some have argued that what they did was immoral. They believe that God would have provided the midwives a way out of their "ethical dilemma"—one that would not have involved a violation of His moral directives. These Christians think that there are never any real conflicts between absolute norms since God will always pave a road that can lead one out of the apparent dilemma. Their position has been called *nonconflicting absolutism* or the *third alternative view*. Other Christians have agreed that the midwives acted immorally, but they have adopted this position for different reasons. These believers contend that the dilemma the midwives faced was real. In such situations, they say, "God knows that no matter what a person does, he will have to break one of His laws. So the Lord commands that he violate the directive that will produce the lesser evil and then plead for God's forgiveness of his sin. In the case of the midwives, since they chose the lesser evil, God rewarded them." This position has been named *conflicting absolutism* or the *lesser evil view*. Yet another group of Christians have held that the Hebrew midwives were absolutely right in what they did. These thinkers argue that when God's laws come into conflict, a person is morally obligated to obey the higher law and morally exempt from keeping the lower law. Thus, when the midwives obeyed the higher command of saving lives, they did not sin. That is why God blessed them without rebuking their lie. This ethical position has been called *graded absolutism* or the *greater good view*. If you would like to probe further into these practical issues, then we would encourage you to consult the sources listed below. They will help you explore the biblical bases and ethical ramifications of the three Christian positions we have briefly explained.

- **The Third Alternative View.**

    Geisler, Norman L., ed. *What Augustine Says.* Grand Rapids: Baker Book House, 1982. See chapter 9 for a clear outline of Augustine's ethical perspective.

    Murray, John. *Principles of Conduct.* Grand Rapids: William B. Eerdmans Publishing Co., 1957.

- **The Lesser Evil View.**
  Carnell, Edward John. *Christian Commitment: An Apologetic.* Grand Rapids: Baker Book House, 1957. See pp. 223–43.
  Fletcher, Joseph, and Montgomery, John Warwick. *Situation Ethics.* Minneapolis: Bethany Fellowship, Inc., 1972. In this dialogue, the Christian theologian Montgomery lays bare his own ethical position and contrasts it with Fletcher's situational ethic.
- **The Greater Good View.**
  Geisler, Norman L. *The Christian Ethic of Love.* Contemporary Evangelical Perspectives. Grand Rapids: Zondervan Publishing House, 1973.
  Geisler, Norman L. *Options in Contemporary Christian Ethics.* Grand Rapids: Baker Book House, 1981. Here Geisler provides excellent summaries of the other two Christian positions as well as a clear presentation and defense of his own view.

Born After Midnight
Exodus 2:1–10

In the seventh chapter of the Book of Acts, we find Moses' life divided into three forty-year segments. His first forty years were spent in Egypt, where the Hebrews were experiencing their darkest days. There he was nursed by his mother at home and educated by Egyptian teachers (vv. 20–28). He spent the next forty years as a shepherd in a foreign land (vv. 29–30a). Then during the final forty years of his life, Moses served God by leading His people out of Egypt, into the wilderness, and up to the border of Canaan (vv. 30b–44). The three periods of his life have also been described this way: Moses spent his first forty years thinking that he was a somebody, his middle years learning that he was a nobody, and his later years discovering what mighty deeds God could perform through a nobody. Certainly Moses was a great man of God. But we will see repeatedly throughout our study that he was very much like each of us—flawed in character and in need of God's strength. In this lesson we will be introduced to some of the dramatic events surrounding his birth and childhood growth. We will see how God used the strong faith of Moses' parents to preserve him for a future mission of deliverance.

I. Moses' Home.

In the previous lesson we learned that Moses was born into a hostile environment. Egypt was ruled by an anti-Semitic despot. The name of this Pharaoh was either Amenhotep I (1545–1526 B.C.) or Thutmose I (1526–1512 B.C.).* He was executing a plan of severe oppression against the Hebrew people that included forced labor and male infanticide (Exod. 1:8–22). During this bleak hour in Hebrew history, Moses was born (Exod. 2:1–2). His father's name was Amram and his mother was Jochebed, Amram's aunt (Exod. 6:20). This Levite couple already had two other children by the time Moses came along. The oldest child was a girl called Miriam (Exod. 15:20). She was probably seven to twelve years older than Moses. The other child's name was Aaron. He was three years the senior of Moses and the one who later became Moses' right-hand man when they confronted Pharaoh over the release of the Hebrews from Egypt (Exod. 6:20, 7:7). After the birth of Moses, his mother "saw that he was beautiful" (Exod. 2:2b). The Hebrew term for *beautiful* suggests that young Moses was truly attractive and well formed. In this case, the word may also convey that Jochebed saw or sensed something special about their new child—perhaps that he was to play a unique role in God's plan for His people (cf. Acts 7:20). At any rate, for the first three months of Moses' childhood, Jochebed kept him hidden away (Exod. 2:2b). Since Moses was a newborn Hebrew

*John D. Hannah, "Exodus," in *The Bible Knowledge Commentary,* edited by John F. Walvoord and Roy B. Zuck (Wheaton: Victor Books, 1985), p. 109.

male, his very life was in jeopardy as a result of Pharaoh's extermination edict (Exod. 1:22). The fact that Moses' parents violated the king's command in order to save their son displays the reverence they had for the Heavenly Lord over the Egyptian lord (cf. Heb. 11:23).

II. Moses' Protection.

There is no doubt that it must have been extremely difficult to hide a newborn for three months. Eventually, however, Jochebed and Amram could conceal Moses no longer (Exod. 2:3a). So Jochebed initiated a clever plan designed to spare her son's life. She either constructed or purchased a basket made out of papyrus and "covered it over with tar and pitch" so it would be watertight (v. 3a). After placing Moses in the basket, she nestled it securely "among the reeds by the bank of the Nile" (v. 3b). Here the water was shallow, and the current was too weak to carry the basket away. Ironically, Jochebed's action was, to a certain degree, in compliance with Pharaoh's edict to cast every Hebrew male newborn into the Nile River (Exod. 1:22). However, while the Egyptian ruler would have had Moses murdered, Jochebed's plan was to have the daughter of Pharaoh save her son. So she set the basket in an area of the Nile that was frequently used by Pharaoh's daughter for bathing. Then she had Moses' sister, Miriam, stand at a distance so that she could both keep an eye on Moses and step into the scene at just the right moment (Exod. 2:4). As the account unfolds, we can readily see that Jochebed's plan of faith worked flawlessly. When Pharaoh's daughter "came down to bathe at the Nile, . . . she saw the basket among the reeds and sent her maid, and she brought it to her" (v. 5). Once this member of the royal family saw the child and heard him crying, she took "pity on him" even though she realized that the boy was a Hebrew (v. 6). This must have relieved both Miriam and Jochebed immensely, for they had no assurance that Pharaoh's daughter would not kill Moses. At the proper moment, Miriam approached the daughter of Pharaoh and asked, " 'Shall I go and call a nurse for you from the Hebrew women, that she may nurse the child for you?' " (v. 7). The Egyptian woman gave her permission. "So the girl went and called the child's mother" (v. 8). Once Miriam returned with Jochebed, "Pharaoh's daughter said to her, 'Take this child away and nurse him for me and I shall give you your wages' " (v. 9a). What a deal! Not only was Jochebed reunited with her son, but she also was told that she would be paid for raising him.

> ### Some Personal Application
>
> Before we move on to the rest of the story, let's draw out a truth that is woven throughout this passage. It is clear that Jochebed exercised great faith and inner courage by hiding young Moses and setting him in the Nile. However, it is also obvious that her

faith was accompanied by a well-thought-out plan which she executed with tremendous skill. Put another way, she was convinced that putting her trust in God involved thinking, planning, and applying on her part. And she was right. The approach to life that says "Let go and let God" is a wrong one. The biblical principle is "Get going with God." Our faith should be active, not passive. It should incorporate foresight and wisdom in its application, not simply hindsight and wishful thinking.

III. Moses' Childhood.

The text goes on to tell us that Jochebed took baby Moses from Pharaoh's daughter and nursed him (v. 9b). And although the passage does not specify how long Jochebed took care of Moses, we can discern from verse 10 and from the adoption customs in Egypt that she probably raised him until his third or fourth birthday.† At any rate, we can be certain that Jochebed reared Moses during the most impressionable years of his childhood. In these few years, Moses must have learned a good deal about the Lord, faith, and his genealogical heritage. This would explain these comments in the Book of Hebrews: "By faith Moses, when he had grown up, refused to be called the son of Pharaoh's daughter; choosing rather to endure ill-treatment with the people of God, than to enjoy the passing pleasures of sin" (Heb. 11:24–25). As we can see, his mother made good use of the short time she had with him.

IV. Moses' Adoption.

Eventually, Jochebed had to give up her son to Pharaoh's daughter. At that juncture, the child was adopted into the royal family and given the name *Moses,* which means "to draw out." Apparently, he received this name because he had been taken out of the Nile River (Exod. 2:10). His stay in the Egyptian court lasted just shy of forty years. During this period, " 'Moses was educated in all the learning of the Egyptians, and he [became] a man of power in words and deeds' " (Acts 7:22). The irony of all of this is that the same child who was nurtured, raised, and educated by Pharaoh's daughter became the instrument God used to bring the royal family to its knees.

V. Your Life.

At times, you may feel as if you had been "born after midnight." Perhaps you were brought into this world during a desperate time in your family's life. Or maybe you have wished that you had been born in another city, to other parents, or under different circumstances so

---

†W. H. Grispen, *Exodus,* translated by Ed van der Maas, Bible Student's Commentary series (Grand Rapids: Regency Reference Library, Zondervan Publishing House, 1982), p. 41.

that your present situation might be more favorable. Rest assured from the life of Moses that what you may deem an ill-timed birth is not considered as such in God's eyes. He has His hand on your life. He wants to do great things through you. And He has designed the experiences of your life to help prepare you for the challenges ahead. So continue to look at your situation through the eyes of heaven. As you do, you will find yourself better able to face and overcome even the most difficult days.

Living Insights

Study One

Put yourself in the place of the main characters in this story—Moses, his mother Jochebed, and Pharaoh's daughter. It's not difficult to imagine the intensity of their emotions, is it? Let's try to uncover some of these feelings.

- Write out Exodus 2:1–10 *in your own words.* Use this assignment as a chance to get into the meanings of the words and the feelings they convey. You will find this passage coming to life as you employ the art of *paraphrasing.* Conclude this study by reading your paraphrase aloud. Then thank the Lord for your findings in this great portion of Scripture.

Living Insights

Study Two

There's a definite application to be made from this study. Whether you would consider yourself to have been born after midnight or under the noonday sun, there is a couple who deserves your thanks—*your parents.*

- When was the last time that you showed some appreciation to your parents for their impact on your life? If your mother and father have passed away, use this time to pray verbally or in writing, telling God what you appreciated in your folks. If your parents are still alive, imagine a creative way to say "thank you." Some ideas you might consider are a phone call, a card or letter, a night out on the town, or a special cassette or videotape of your thoughts. The only rule is this: Keep all negative thoughts out of your message. Instead, make it positive, gracious, and most of all, thankful.

God's Will, My Way
Exodus 2:10–15, Acts 7:21–29

In many situations the will of God is clearly discernible, leaving little room for man's interpretation. For example, we realize from Scripture that the Lord wants us to raise our children in a way that fits their character and abilities (Prov. 22:6). This process includes instructing our children about life from God's perspective (Deut. 4:9–10, 11:18–19). The problem arises when we try to achieve this goal our way rather than God's. In other words, we often aim for the right goal, but we use the wrong means. The Lord's desire is that we match His will with His way. Any other approach is doomed to fail. A man named Moses learned this lesson well over three thousand years ago. We can benefit from his mistake if we will only heed the application embedded in his story. So let's turn our attention to a recorded failure in order that we might discover a method for success.

I. **The Egyptian Lifestyle** (Exodus 2:10, Acts 7:21–22).
   In the previous lesson we learned that after Pharaoh's daughter discovered Moses, she unknowingly turned him over to his mother for his early upbringing (Exod. 2:5–8). But once Moses had grown to be a certain age—possibly three or four years old—Jochebed returned him "to Pharaoh's daughter, and he became her son" (v. 10a). For the next several years, Moses the Hebrew was brought up as an Egyptian. The biblical text summarizes this period of his life through four facts. Let's take a few moments to examine each one.
   A. **Given a New Name** (Exod. 2:10b). As a Hebrew child adopted into the Egyptian royal family, the young boy was renamed "Moses" by Pharaoh's daughter. This shows us that an attempt was made from the beginning of Moses' adoption to conform him to an Egyptian identity and lifestyle.
   B. **Nurtured in the Court** (Acts 7:21). This New Testament reference tells us that Pharaoh's daughter nurtured Moses " 'as her own son.' " The Greek word translated *nurtured* means "to educate, rear." Moses was raised as any child in the royal family would be. He was given a majestic suite, tutored in court life and protocol, advised on cultural and traditional matters, and instructed in the finest arts of his day. In fact, many historians believe that he was being groomed for the throne of Egypt.
   C. **Educated in Egyptian Schools** (Acts 7:22a). Since Moses had become a member of the wealthy ruling class, he had access to the best education in Egypt. This was found at the Temple of the Sun. Some historians have referred to this learning center as the Oxford University of the ancient world. Here a child was trained in a rigorous course of study that included being educated in the reading and writing of hieroglyphic and hieratic

scripts. Moses would have also received instruction on Egyptian "theology, astronomy, medicine, mathematics, and other subjects, in virtually everything that was part of the intellectual domain of the civilized world of that time." * This is why the biblical text records that " 'Moses was educated in all the learning of the Egyptians.' "

D. Respected in the Land (Acts 7:22b). By the time of Moses' fortieth birthday, he had become " 'a man of power in words and deeds.' " His intellectual acumen coupled with his oratory skills and practical wisdom had brought him a reputation of renown throughout the nation of Egypt.

II. Operation Self-will (Exodus 2:11–15a, Acts 7:23–29).

In spite of Moses' maturity, education, wisdom, and stature, he initiated a plan for delivering the Hebrews that could only lead to ruin. The central problem with his idea was that it was *his* plan, *not God's.* Moses attempted to perform God's will his way. As we shall see, the scriptural account suggests that Moses knew he was God's choice for leading the Hebrews out of Egypt. However, he apparently decided on his own when and how the Exodus was to take place. As we see what he did and the consequences that followed, we will begin to learn how to prevent such a fleshly operation from being enacted in our lives.

A. The idea was initiated by Moses, not God (Exod. 2:11b–12, Acts 7:23). In Acts 7, we read that when Moses " 'was approaching the age of forty, it entered his mind to visit his brethren, the sons of Israel' " (v. 23). Rather than waiting on God, Moses set in motion a premature plan for carrying out God's will. His scheme began with murder:

> He went out to his brethren and looked on their hard labors; and he saw an Egyptian beating a Hebrew, one of his brethren. So he looked this way and that, and when he saw there was no one around, he struck down the Egyptian and hid him in the sand. (Exod. 2:11b–12)

B. The procedure was energized by the flesh (Exod. 2:12). We are never told that God commanded Moses to go out among the Hebrews and slay an abusive Egyptian. Instead, we read that the idea originated with Moses and was enacted through his own power. Just before he killed the Egyptian, he looked in every direction but up (Exod. 2:12a). He failed to consult God, ignoring the wisdom and power available to him. Even though his motives were probably pure (cf. Acts 7:24b–25), his method certainly was not. Perhaps Moses first realized this after he killed the Egyptian. For it was at that time he tried to hide his deed by

*W. H. Grispen, *Exodus,* translated by Ed van der Maas, Bible Student's Commentary series (Grand Rapids: Regency Reference Library, Zondervan Publishing House, 1982), p. 41.

burying the slain victim in the sand (Exod. 2:12b). Spiritually speaking, acts committed in the flesh will often need to be hidden in some way. We can avoid the deceit and guilt that accompany such cover-ups by living in the Spirit rather than in the flesh (cf. Rom. 8).

C. **The act led to confusion and failure** (Exod. 2:13–14, Acts 7:25–29a). Moses " 'supposed that his brethren understood that God was granting them deliverance through him' " (Acts 7:25a). He knew that God wanted him to free the Hebrews, and he apparently thought that the Hebrews realized that as well. But the text informs us that the Israelites " 'did not understand' " what Moses was doing (v. 25b). Because it was not yet God's time for their deliverance, they were confused by Moses' murdering of the Egyptian. So when Moses went back out to the Hebrews the next day and tried to reconcile two who were fighting with one another (v. 26), he received an unexpected response: " 'The one who was injuring his neighbor pushed him [Moses] away, saying, 'Who made you a ruler and judge over us? You do not mean to kill me as you killed the Egyptian yesterday, do you?' " (v. 27). At that juncture Moses became "afraid, and said, 'Surely the matter has become known' " (Exod. 2:14b). The people did not rally around Moses as their leader. His plan had only brought confusion and failure, not peace and success. Whenever we try to initiate and enact ideas by our own strength, we will eventually find ourselves defeated like Moses. However, if we will submit to God's plan and carry it out His way, then we can only succeed.

D. **The plan created unbearable conditions** (Exod. 2:15, Acts 7:29b). When Pharaoh heard about what Moses had done, he tried to kill him. Fearing for his life, "Moses fled from the presence of Pharaoh and settled in the land of Midian; and he sat down by a well" (Exod. 2:15). Because he had acted apart from God's will in method and timing, he was forced to leave his surroundings of luxury for a desert of poverty. There, in Midian, the pride of Egypt sat down next to a well in order to rest and lick his wounds.

III. **Some Lingering Lessons.**
Spiritual principles abound in this tragic story. Among them, two stand out as particularly essential for our walk with God.

A. **When the self-life has run its course, we find ourselves settling in a desert.** Fleshly actions will invariably lead to spiritual dryness. At that point, we usually stop and wonder if God will ever use us again.

14

B. When the self-life sits down, the well of a new life is near. Highly qualified and self-driven people seldom sit down long enough to get in tune with God. But when they finally come to their wits' end, they are ready to find cool refreshment in the abundant well of God. And it is never far away. Indeed, it can usually be found right next to them, just waiting to quench their spiritual thirst.

Living Insights

Study One

We are fortunate to have a passage in the New Testament that underscores what we're learning in the Old Testament. Turn to Acts 7 for a look at a sermon delivered by the Church's first martyr, Stephen.

- Acts 7:20–44 covers the life of Moses through the perspective of Stephen. Use these twenty-five verses as the basis for your personal *outline* of Moses' life. Look for the main points about his life as well as those incidents that might be better described as sub-points. You will probably find it helpful to read the entire passage first before breaking it down into appropriate sections.

An Outline of Moses' Life—Acts 7:20–44

At the heart of this lesson was a section we titled "Operation Self-will." Did you notice the progression that led to unbearable conditions? The four points we gave are stated below in a slightly different form. Personalize them by giving examples of how these stages have manifested themselves in your life. Your illustrations could be drawn from past incidents or even from current experiences.

- An idea was initiated by me, not God.
- A procedure was energized by my flesh.
- An act I performed led to confusion and failure.
- A plan I enacted led to unbearable conditions.

Lessons Learned from Failure

Exodus 2:11–25, Psalm 119:67,71

Have you ever heard anyone say "If you will just accept Jesus Christ as your Savior, then all your problems will be solved"? This is a nice thought, but it's not true. Christians are never promised a life on earth filled with success and ease. In fact, the Bible assumes and even teaches that failure and discomfort will be part of a believer's spiritual growth. A prime example of a person who failed miserably before succeeding magnificently is Moses. After taking God's will into his own hands, he ended up fleeing Egypt to spare his life because he had murdered a man. Feeling humiliated, ashamed, embarrassed, and worthless, he sat down by a well in the midst of a rocky, barren desert. But his mistake was not made in vain. He learned a great deal from his failure ... and so can we. So let's take some time to reflect on our failures as we think back upon his. By doing so, we can learn how to turn even our worst disasters into building blocks for future successes.

I.   Basic Principles on Failure (Psalm 119:67, 71).

Before we fix our attention on Moses' first recorded error, let's glean two principles concerning failure from these verses in the Psalter. Although the psalmist uses the word *affliction* to convey pain and hurt, the idea of failure with its accompanying feelings of defeat and dejection are also grounded in the term's meaning. With this in mind, let's consider the key truths he presents.

A.   Experiencing failure promotes an obedient life. The psalmist states this principle in these words:

Before I was afflicted I went astray,
But now I keep Thy word. (v. 67)

When we come to the end of a road where we have been bruised, broken, and humiliated, we often sense a renewed drive to get back on track with God. We know that the path we took was a dead end. We then stand before our Lord humble in heart and willing to obey.

B.   Experiencing failure prompts a teachable spirit. It is amazing how a blow to our plans can help us lift up our voices to God and pay more attention to His answers. The ancient psalmist found this to be true in his life. That is why he penned this thought:

It is good for me that I was afflicted,
That I may learn Thy statutes. (v. 71)

Failure can bring a sensitivity to divine instruction that would probably not exist in the presence of success. Why? Because brokenness tends to strip away the most impregnable barrier to teachability—pride. But once that is gone, we can hear God

17

more clearly and learn from Him more effectively. And those two elements are integral to a successful Christian life.

II. Specific Lessons from Failure (Exodus 2:11–15).
We are now ready to look at a biblical personification of failure—Moses. These verses from Exodus 2 record Moses' attempt to achieve God's will his way. The outcome, of course, was a murdered Egyptian and a misunderstood and fearful Moses. Rather than leading the Hebrews to freedom, Moses ended up confused, tired, and shaken in the desert land of Midian. There he sat next to a well, probably feeling as if God would never again use him in any significant way. There is little doubt that Moses used this time to reflect on his grave mistake. If he did, then he probably learned at least four lessons that later helped him to become one of Israel's greatest leaders. Let's peruse them together.

A. Spiritual ends are not achieved by carnal means. Moses acted on his own when "he struck down the Egyptian and hid him in the sand" (v. 12b). As a consequence, the execution of his scheme led to sin instead of deliverance. It could not have ended any other way.

B. Timing is as important as action. God's plans must be enacted at the appropriate times. If Moses knew this, he chose to ignore it. Rather than waiting on the Lord to move him into leadership, he prematurely pushed his way into the position. And the result was that no one followed him (vv. 13–14). He needed to learn that waiting on God is the mark of wisdom and strength, not foolishness and weakness.

C. Hiding the wrong done does not erase it. When Moses tried to hide his murderous act by burying the Egyptian in the sand (v. 12b), he exercised a muscle of sin that had been in man since Adam and Eve. After they had eaten of the forbidden tree in the Garden of Eden, they tried to cover up their sin by clothing themselves and hiding from God (Gen. 3:1–8). Some time later their son Cain mimicked their response when he buried his brother Abel after murdering him (Gen. 4:8–11). In both cases, the cover-up failed and divine judgment followed (Gen. 3:9–19, 4:9–12). Indeed, the attempt to conceal sin only delayed its discovery and intensified the severity of the failure. The same occurred with Moses and still transpires in our lives today.

D. Spiritual leadership is God-appointed, not self-assumed. Moses had an incredible resumé. He was raised in the right neighborhood, schooled in the best institution, respected as a powerful speaker and leader, recognized as a man of principle, and to top it all off, physically attractive (Exod. 2:2, 10; Acts 7:20–22; Heb. 11:23–26). But simply because he had been raised to be involved in national leadership did not mean that he was ready to take the reigns of spiritual leadership. No one can adequately lead God's people until they become consistent followers of God. Moses apparently thought that his job was to take God's place rather than to obediently follow His lead.

III. Strategic Changes after Failure (Exodus 2:16–25).

Did Moses learn from his mistake? He certainly did! Eventually, he stepped away from the well of reflection on wrong and moved toward a life of obedience to God. These verses from Exodus 2 show us three changes that took place in Moses as a result of what he learned through failure.

A. The Development of a Servant's Attitude. When seven women came to the well "to water their father's flock," the Pharaoh-elect of Egypt "stood up and helped them, and watered their flock" (vv. 16–17). Moses the leader took the first step to becoming Moses the servant.

B. The Willingness to Be Obscure. The man of Egyptian royalty accepted the invitation of Jethro the priest, who was also called Reuel, to become a live-in member of his shepherding household (Exod. 2:18–21, 3:1). After he married Zipporah, one of Jethro's daughters, "she gave birth to a son." Moses "named him *Gershom* [which means, "a stranger there"], for he said, 'I have been a sojourner in a foreign land' " (Exod. 2:21b–22, emphasis added). Moses was willing to live away from the limelight and in the shadows of an obscure home in a barren desert.

C. The Ability to Rest and Rely on God. The final verses of Exodus 2 paint a bleak and tragic scene with God as the single ray of hope.

> Now it came about in the course of those many days that the king of Egypt died. And the sons of Israel sighed because of the bondage, and they cried out; and their cry for help because of their bondage rose up to God. So God heard their groaning; and God remembered His covenant with Abraham, Isaac, and Jacob. And God saw the sons of Israel, and God took notice of them. (vv. 23–25)

Did you observe that no mention is made of Moses? Although he probably continued receiving reports of the Hebrews' misery, he did not run back and initiate another premature attempt to free them. Instead, he spent forty years raising a family and pasturing a flock, while trusting God to deliver the Hebrews in

His way and according to His timetable. Moses had definitely
learned his lesson.

IV. Concluding Thoughts about Failure.

We usually continue to make mistakes because we do not stop to learn
from them. This sends us into a tailspin that often drains our strength
and shatters our confidence. It is unfortunate that God must often
bring us to the end of our resources before we will listen to and heed
His Word. But the good news is that we do not have to remain bruised
and broken. We can use our failures to move closer to our divine
Healer and Counselor. This can be accomplished by taking some time
to reflect on and learn from our mistakes. However, if we keep stepping
into the same self-made traps, then our feelings of despair, loneliness,
and uselessness will most likely increase, and our walk with God will
continue to suffer. The alternatives are clear. And the choice between
them is ours. Which option will *you* take today?

Living Insights

Study One

In this study we saw Moses as a personification of failure. We also
observed some of what he learned as a result of his mistakes. Since we
all err from time to time, let's take this opportunity to probe further
into Moses' failure so that we can better learn how to handle ours.

- Copy the following chart into your notebook. Then read through
  Exodus 2:11–25. In the left column of this chart, jot down all the
  key words you find in the passage. Once you have done this, see if
  you can discover the meaning of each word from its context. If you
  cannot, then consult a good Bible dictionary—such as *Unger's
  Bible Dictionary* (Chicago: Moody Press, rev. ed., 1966)—and write
  the definition it gives in the center column. Finally, in the last
  column of the chart, give a helpful phrase indicating the
  significance of each word to the story as a whole.

Exodus 2:11–25		
Key Words	Definitions	Significance

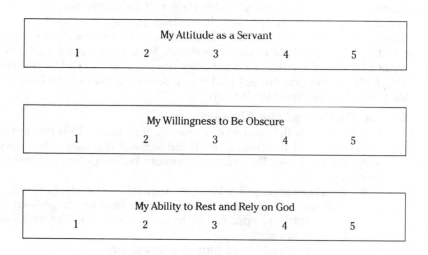

Living Insights

The story about Moses doesn't end with failure. As a matter of fact, we have observed three strategic changes that occurred in his life *after* he took matters into his own hands. Use the following scale to evaluate your score in the areas where Moses matured. The number five indicates the best, and number one stands for the worst.

My Attitude as a Servant				
1	2	3	4	5

My Willingness to Be Obscure				
1	2	3	4	5

My Ability to Rest and Rely on God				
1	2	3	4	5

• How did you do? Wrap up this survey by jotting down two or three simple projects you can accomplish over the next few days to help you further exemplify these traits in your life.

21

The Desert: School of Self-discovery

Exodus 2:21–22, 3:1; Acts 7:29–30a

For the better part of forty years, Moses lived in a palace. While there, he received the finest academic training available so that he could reach the pinnacle of human achievement. But he needed more education before he could qualify as God's man of deliverance. He lacked a lengthy postgraduate course at God's "university"—the desert. This study was designed to humble Moses through obscurity, hone him through time, and purify him through suffering. As we will see, God's training program was thorough and effective. Because of his desert experience, Moses developed qualities that cannot be gained by reading textbooks or sitting at the feet of professors. This forty-year course turned him into a seasoned man of the Lord, ready for the task of spiritual leadership.

I. God's Use of the Desert.

Before we turn the spotlight on Moses, let's place it on two passages in the Book of Deuteronomy. There we will discover some specific ways the Lord uses the desert to prepare believers for His benevolent purpose.

A. Deuteronomy 32:10. Although this verse deals specifically with the nation of Israel—referred to here as "Jacob"—it has a wider spiritual application to each one of us. The first part of the passage says,

"He [God] found him in a desert land,
And in the howling waste of a wilderness."

The Hebrew word for *desert* comes from a verb which means "to speak." The desert is not a place where God is absent and silent. We may feel that it is, but in fact He is actively seeking us and striving to communicate to us in even the most barren experiences. Whether our desert takes the form of confinement, ill health, a broken romance, failure at work, or even the death of a loved one, God is with us desiring to see us through. This fact is clearly conveyed in the rest of the verse. While Israel was wandering in the desert,

"He encircled him, He cared for him,
He guarded him as the pupil of His eye."

In our most lonely, desperate struggles, the divine Shepherd will not abandon us. Instead, He will come to our aid in a way that will far surpass the help He renders in the easier moments of life.

B. Deuteronomy 8:2. The words of this verse were originally spoken to Israel at the end of her wilderness wanderings. But the truths they convey apply to our difficult times as well. Indeed, they explain the purpose of our desert experiences. Read the passage thoughtfully: " 'And you shall remember all the way which the Lord your God has led you in the wilderness these forty years, [so] that He might humble you, testing you, to know what was in your heart, whether you would keep His commandments or not.' " This verse is not teaching that God needed to observe Israel in the desert in order to see what she would do. Since the Lord is all-knowing, He knew before the world was even created how the Hebrews would respond to their trek through the wilderness. Thus, their desert experience was willed by God for their benefit, not His. The Lord uses our bleak times for a similar purpose. Through them, our masks are peeled away so that we may discover who we really are. And with our strengths and weaknesses vividly exposed, we are more apt to stand humbly before God than we otherwise would. Furthermore, it is at this stage of nakedness that the Lord performs some of His best refining work in our lives.

II. Moses' Time in the Desert.

Moving from Deuteronomy to Exodus 3:1 and Acts 7:29–30a, we pass from Israel's experience in the desert to Moses'. In these passages we learn a good deal about the difficult course he took and the faculty members who taught him through it.

A. His Location. As we have mentioned before, Moses fled to and settled in "the land of Midian" (Exod. 2:15). Although its exact location is disputed, it is generally agreed that Midian lay to the south of Canaan and included the northwestern portion of the Sinai Peninsula as well as Mount Sinai.* This is a flat, barren area covered mostly by sand, shrubs, and rocks. It has certainly never been considered a desirable place to vacation or retire.

B. His Vocation. Within this desolate land, Moses spent much of his time "pasturing the flock of Jethro his father-in-law" (Exod. 3:1a). We also know that while living in Midian, Moses and his wife, Zipporah, had two sons (Acts 7:29). So here was a man who was educated by the finest Egyptian teachers, one who had enjoyed a life of luxury and political influence. But now he was living in a wasteland, trying to meet his family's many needs by working as a shepherd for his father-in-law. In comparison to his past, Moses was not only in a physical desert but in a vocational one as well.

*For more information on this, see the following sources: Carl Edwin Armerding, "Midian; Midianites," in *The New International Dictionary of Biblical Archaeology,* edited by E. M. Blaiklock and R. K. Harrison (Grand Rapids: Regency Reference Library, Zondervan Publishing House, 1983), p. 314; "Midian," in *The New Westminster Dictionary of the Bible,* edited by Henry Snyder Gehman (Philadelphia: The Westminster Press, 1970), p. 618.

C. His Education. Moses' course of study in the "School of Self-discovery" included the instruction given by four professors. These teachers were commissioned by God to prepare Moses for the last forty years of his life as the human leader of Israel. Let's take this opportunity to meet them.

1. **Dr. Obscurity.** He taught Moses, who had been a somebody, how to cope with being a nobody in man's eyes. He accomplished this by putting Moses in charge of a flock of dumb, dirty sheep. And it wasn't even Moses' flock but his father-in-law's! The man who had lived in the limelight as a national leader was reduced to living with and working for a relative in the middle of a desert (Exod. 2:21, 3:1). Now that's the work of obscurity!

2. **Dr. Time.** He helped Moses learn how to wait. Before settling in Midian, Moses had become impatient with God's timetable for deliverance. So he tried to speed matters up by murdering an Egyptian. Apparently, his plan was that this act would cause the Hebrews to rally around him so that they could overpower the Egyptians and leave the country (cf. Acts 7:23–25). But his impetuousness only led to his departure from Egypt as a fugitive from justice (v. 29a). Moses needed to understand the value of patience. So God gave him the opportunity to learn it by making him wait forty years before calling him to that task again (v. 30a).

3. **Dr. Solitude.** This instructor educated Moses in the profundity of silence and solitude. The desert is a quiet and lonely place that encourages thought and reflection. There Moses had the alone-time required to deepen his understanding of himself and the Lord.

4. **Dr. Discomfort.** He used the harsh environment of the Midian desert to strengthen Moses physically and spiritually. Without this training, Moses may not have been able to lead the Hebrews through the trials they were to face in the wilderness for forty years.

III. Your Response to the Desert.

Most likely, your desert is not a geographical location. You may be suffering through a spiritual, physical, emotional, or relational desert. Whatever the case, God wants to use it to help you discover yourself and His all-sufficient resources. But you will not learn the lessons He has prepared for you if you respond to your situation inappropriately. There are three ways you can respond, but only one will see you through God's school of self-discovery.

A. **"I don't need it."** This is the reaction of fear or pride. If you respond in this manner, then you are saying in effect that anyone but you should have to pass through the desert. No instruction can be received with this poor attitude.

B. **"I'm tired of it."** This response usually comes after a good deal of fatigue or anxiety has been felt in the midst of one's struggle. It's certainly not abnormal, but it's more conducive to self-pity than to self-discovery.

C. **"I accept it."** This is the response that promotes the greatest degree of learning. If you find yourself in the desert, then don't try to fight it, run away from it, or fall victim to it. Instead, turn your situation over to God. Trust that He has matters under control. And realize that He has designed it for your benefit, not your detriment. This will give you the perspective you need for learning the valuable lessons He desires to teach you.

🌺 *Living Insights*

Study One

In God's master plan, He prepares some of His children through the difficulties they face in the desert. Those of us who have been there have come to realize that the desert experience is one of barrenness, discomfort, and loneliness. Let's look further into God's Word to discover more about life in the wilderness.

- The serious Bible student's best friend is his exhaustive concordance. It records all the appearances of each word found in Scripture. Locate a Bible concordance and look up two words: *desert* and *wilderness.* In your copy of the following chart, list the references given. Then read each passage and write down the descriptions that are mentioned. When you're finished, you'll have a much better understanding of what God means when He uses these terms.

Word Study		
Terms	References	Descriptions
Desert		
Wilderness		

🏇 *Living Insights*

The desert is the school of self-discovery. There God teaches us about ourselves and our relationship to Him. How about recording some of the lessons we have learned? Use the example below to fill in the specifics of a desert experience from your past or present. Then commit yourself to review and update it periodically so that you don't forget what He has taught you.

My Desert Experience

Event:

Date:

Place:

Time:

How God Has Used Obscurity:

How God Has Used Time:

How God Has Used Solitude:

How God Has Used Discomfort:

Burning Bridges
or Burning Bushes
Exodus 3:1–10

God specializes in restoring failures. The Bible is full of stories about people who God used in mighty ways even after they had failed miserably. For example, Jacob lived many of his days as a deceiver and a cheat. However, the Lord preserved the Hebrew people through him (Gen. 25:19–50:14). The prophet Jonah was utilized by God to save the capital city of Assyria from destruction. And this revival took place only after the Lord persuaded disobedient Jonah to follow through with his appointed, evangelistic mission (see the Book of Jonah). Another failure God used was Moses. We have already seen how his premature plan led him to shepherd a flock of sheep rather than deliver the descendants of Jacob. And we have imagined how dejected and useless he must have felt during his forty-year stay in the desert. Was he to die feeling lonely and forgotten? No. In this lesson, we will see how the Lord can start mending our brokenness and use us again for His service.

I. The Day.
The third chapter of Exodus opens with a simple description of what had become the common practice of Moses: "Now Moses was pasturing the flock of Jethro his father-in-law, the priest of Midian; and he led the flock to the west side of the wilderness, and came to Horeb, the mountain of God." (v. 1) The day on which the Lord chose to end His forty-year training period with Moses began as just an ordinary day in the desert. There is no indication that God preceded His appearance to Moses with any special phenomena, giving him notice that something unique was about to happen. Rather, this day dawned like any other day in Moses' life.

> *Personal Application:* God's method is the same today. Except in unusual and rare circumstances, the Lord will not warn us that He is about to intervene in a special or miraculous way. Instead, we will usually receive a unique visit from Him when we least expect it—during the humdrum routine of our day. So we need to be always on the alert, for we will seldom know beforehand when He will begin to move us from the ordinary and toward the extraordinary.

II. The Bush.
It's easy to imagine Moses walking beside his flock, shaking the sand out of his sandals from time to time, and trying to keep the sheep from wandering away and getting snagged in briar patches. Then, all

of a sudden, something remarkable occurs. The text describes it this way: "And the angel of the Lord appeared to him in a blazing fire from the midst of a bush; and he looked, and behold, the bush was burning with fire, yet the bush was not consumed. So Moses said, 'I must turn aside now, and see this marvelous sight, why the bush is not burned up.' " (vv. 2–3) The bush Moses saw was nothing special. It was merely one of a vast number of thorny shrubs that covered the desert landscape. But what was happening to the bush was definitely out of the ordinary. After all, Moses knew that a dry plant would not only burn when set on fire, but that it would burn up quickly. This bush, however, was burning without turning to ashes. A sight such as this naturally made Moses curious. So he turned to observe the strange phenomenon.

> **Personal Application:** In the midst of commonplace situations, God will often get our attention by causing an uncommon event to occur. Many times we refer to these special occasions as "coincidences." But these are not mere chance events. They are God's way of tapping us on the shoulder so that we will sit up and listen to what He has to say. We need to be more sensitive to this divine method. Otherwise, we will miss the message that God has for us.

III. The Need.

It was not until Moses turned to look at the burning bush that "God called to him from the midst of the bush, [saying] 'Moses, Moses!' " (v. 4a). At this juncture, Moses still did not know that the Lord was the One who was speaking to him. All he saw was a bush on fire. And what he heard was an unfamiliar, authoritative-sounding voice. So he responded to the call with a simple answer, " 'Here I am' " (v. 4b). Through these words, he indicated both his acknowledgement of the call and his availability to respond further. Then God spoke to him again: " 'Do not come near here; remove your sandals from your feet, for the place on which you are standing is holy ground' " (v. 5). The Lord commanded Moses to consider the piece of desert that he was standing on as sacred. Certainly this directive did not mean that the ground under Moses' feet was morally pure. However, what it did indicate was that this very sand took on special significance because the Lord of creation was speaking to someone who was standing on it. In other words, God's supernatural presence before Moses gave his ordinary surroundings extraordinary status. Then the Lord followed His command with a declaration of His identity: " 'I am the God of your father, the God of Abraham, the God of Isaac, and the God of Jacob' " (v. 6a). When Moses heard this, he realized that the One whom he had failed in Egypt was now facing him in Midian. This struck terror and guilt into his heart. As a result, "Moses hid his face" (v. 6b). But this act of humiliation did not stop the Lord from communicating to Moses. He went on to tell about His awareness of and concern for the Hebrews' oppression in Egypt:

"I have surely seen the affliction of My people who are in Egypt, and have given heed to their cry because of their taskmasters, for I am aware of their sufferings. So I have come down to deliver them from the power of the Egyptians, and to bring them up from that land to a good and spacious land, to a land flowing with milk and honey, to the place of the Canaanite and the Hittite and the Amorite and the Perizzite and the Hivite and the Jebusite. And now, behold, the cry of the sons of Israel has come to Me; furthermore, I have seen the oppression with which the Egyptians are oppressing them." (vv. 7–9)

Personal Application: The Lord wants us to be attentive to His voice and available for His work. This holds true even after we have disappointed Him. He neither gives up on us nor forsakes us. Indeed, when we are going through our darkest days, we can be confident that He is totally aware, thoroughly involved, and completely in control of our situation.

IV. The Call.

After spending forty years of obscurity in Midian as the result of failure, the eighty-year-old Moses heard God commission him to return to Egypt and deliver the Hebrews: " 'Therefore, come now, and I will send you to Pharaoh, so that you may bring My people, the sons of Israel, out of Egypt' " (v. 10). Taking into consideration the events recorded in Exodus 2, we might restate the key thought embedded in the first section of chapter 3 in these words: "Moses," God says, "forty years ago you thought you were some important bush in the land of Egypt. But when you set yourself on fire by initiating an impromptu plan of your own making, you burnt yourself up in a matter of days. By the time you arrived in Midian, you were only a heap of ashes. You obviously thought that you, as the bush, sustained the flame. But you learned that you were wrong. I want you to know that it is I, the Flame, who sustains the bush. And I can choose which bush I desire to use whenever I want. Moses, you are the bush I would like to use. Just as I have set this desert shrub on fire and kept it from being consumed, so I want to set you on fire for My work of deliverance while protecting you from the trials that could destroy you. Are you available for the task?"

Personal Application: Even after we have failed God and think that we are useless, He will return to restore us and call us back into His service. When He does, there are four responses we can make. Only the fourth is the right one. First, *we can run ahead before we are sent.* This response is generally caused by unchecked intensity. Moses chose this option when he was forty years old, and the consequence was disastrous. Second, *we can retreat after we have failed.* Insecurity will often bring this alternative to the surface. Moses exercised this option as well. It led him to a desert experience that lasted forty years. Third, *we can resist when we have been called.* A sense of inferiority usually lies behind this approach. We will discover later that this response was also made by Moses. Fourth, *we can remain available while we wait, and we can respond obediently when we are called.* This is the response of spiritual maturity, and it is the one God is looking for from His people. Which way are you reacting to God's work in your life?

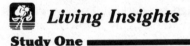 *Living Insights*

Study One ▬▬▬▬▬▬▬▬▬▬▬▬▬▬▬▬▬▬▬▬▬▬▬▬▬▬▬▬▬▬▬

The story of Moses and the burning bush is often brushed aside by most of us. Usually this is so because we're too familiar with it. Many of us have heard this account from childhood, so the freshness of its message has gone stale. Why don't we take a new approach to this event?

- Try reading this narrative in a *different* version. Locate at least one other translation or paraphrase and read Exodus 3:1–10. In this version, what strikes you differently? Try to make three new observations from the passage.

30

🌹 *Living Insights*

Is there a burning bush in your life? Is God attempting to get your attention for an area of service? Let's take some time to talk with God about the day, the bush, the need, and the call in *your* life.

• This time, our "Living Insights" section is reserved for *prayer*. Exodus 3 records a turning point in Moses' life. Is God attempting to communicate the same message to you? Use the four points in our outline below to help you chart out your talk with our Father.

    1. Pray about the day. Has God chosen to speak to you today?

    2. Pray about the bush. Is God trying to get your attention?

    3. Pray about the need. Are you available to meet it?

    4. Pray about the call. Will you heed it?

Who Me, Lord?

Exodus 3:10–4:19

In the previous lesson, we learned that we can respond to God in three negative ways: we can run before we are sent, we can retreat after we have failed, or we can resist when we are called. We have already seen Moses make the first two responses. Here we will view him reacting to God in the third way. What we will discover is that Moses mislearned the lessons in humility he had received. Consequently, he felt so inferior and incompetent that when God called him to return to Egypt, he replied with excuses. We will analyze each excuse Moses gave and each answer God delivered. Through this ancient dialogue, we will learn how we should respond to Him once we have quit resisting His call.

I. God Calls Moses.

Moses had been a fugitive in the land of Midian for forty years—a long time to spend licking the wounds inflicted by failure. Then, without any warning, the Lord spoke to him from a burning bush in the midst of the desert. And of all the things He could have said, He spoke the words that were the hardest for Moses to handle: " 'Therefore, come now, and I will send you to Pharaoh, so that you may bring My people, the sons of Israel, out of Egypt' " (Exod. 3:10). God's plan was simple. Moses was to return to Egypt as the Lord's appointed servant and act as His instrument of deliverance. God did not ask for Moses' advice or seek after his permission; He simply told him to go and do as He had said. But apparently, Moses misconstrued the divine command. He seemed to think that God wanted *him* to be Israel's deliverer. However, the Lord's intention was that Moses be the *instrument* through which He would bring the Hebrews out of Egypt. Because Moses misunderstood, he responded to God's call with a question of resistance: " 'Who am I, that I should go to Pharaoh, and that I should bring the sons of Israel out of Egypt?' " (v. 11). God immediately corrected him with these words of reassurance: " 'Certainly I will be with you, and this shall be the sign to you that it is I who have sent you: when you have brought the people out of Egypt, you shall worship God at this mountain' " (v. 12). This is a reference to Mount Sinai. It is one of a number of granite mountains in the Sinai Peninsula, "the highest of which rise nearly 8000 feet above sea level."* God wanted Moses to know that this huge mountain he was standing by would be the place where he would bring the Hebrews to worship Him. By giving this prophecy, the Lord was making it clear to Moses that he was His choice for the task.

*G. Ernest Wright, *Biblical Archaeology,* rev. and exp. ed. (Philadelphia: The Westminster Press, 1962), p. 63. Pages 62–63 include graphic pictures of Mount Sinai and the barren desert that surrounds it.

II. Moses Resists God.

But Moses did not see himself as God did. Like a stubborn mule rather than an obedient sheep, he tried to convince the Lord that he was not the right person for the job. During his resistance attempt, he gave God four excuses. After each one, God responded with a direct and sufficient answer. Let's take some time to examine each one.

A. Excuse Number One: "I will not have all the answers."
Moses posed a potential scenario to God: " 'Behold, I am going to the sons of Israel, and I shall say to them, "The God of your fathers has sent me to you." Now they may say to me, "What is His name?" What shall I say to them?' " (v. 13). Apparently, Moses was afraid that he would look foolish to the Hebrews if he could not answer their questions. So rather than experiencing some embarrassment, he was electing to remain in Midian with his father-in-law's sheep. *A Personal Note:* It is true that believers are commanded in Scripture to be always "ready to make a defense to every one who asks [them] to give an account for the hope that is in [them]" (1 Pet. 3:15a). But this does not mean that they must know everything before they can talk with anyone. When the Lord calls on us to do something, we should do it. Sometimes He may include further education in His plan for us. But if He doesn't, then we shouldn't try to stall His work by pleading ignorance.

B. Answer Number One: "But you will have all of Me."
The Lord's response to Moses included a lesson on His nature. Notice what He said:

"I AM WHO I AM"; and He said, "Thus you shall say to the sons of Israel, 'I AM has sent me to you.' " And God, furthermore, said to Moses, "Thus you shall say to the sons of Israel, 'The Lord, the God of your fathers, the God of Abraham, the God of Isaac, and the God of Jacob, has sent me to you.' This is My name forever, and this is My memorial-name to all generations." (Exod. 3:14–15)

In the Hebrew language, the divine name *I AM* is only written with the consonants *YHWH.* Many Bible scholars believe that this name was probably pronounced "Yähwĕh." However, no one is certain about its pronunciation, because the Jews came to revere it so highly that they stopped verbalizing it. In place of this word, they pronounced the term *Adonai,* which means "Lord." The name translated *I AM* comes from the Hebrew verb for "to be." Thus, the name *YHWH* is a declaration of God's eternal and immutable self-existence. He is pure being. Nothing has brought or could bring Him into existence. Nor could anything ever cause Him to cease to be. He has always existed and will always exist because He *is* existence. There is no other attribute of God that better stands as the summation of His nature than this one. Moses apparently realized that, for he did not pursue his first excuse any further. He understood that the living God was offering Himself in all of His fullness to him, an eighty-year-old shepherd.

C. **Excuse Number Two: "I may not receive all of their respect."** Moses stated this new excuse in these words: " 'What if they will not believe me, or listen to what I say? For they may say, "The Lord has not appeared to you" ' " (Exod. 4:1). Here Moses displayed his fear of being ridiculed and his lack of personal prestige. Indeed, he showed himself to be a worrier. His excuse begins with the words *what if,* displaying that he was overly anxious about a purely hypothetical situation. And Moses voiced this concern after the Lord had told him that the Hebrews would follow his leadership (Exod. 3:18).

D. **Answer Number Two: "But you will have all of My power."** God demonstrated to Moses how He would ensure that both the Hebrews and the Egyptians would heed his words. The Lord said that He would accomplish this end by giving three miraculous signs. The first two were performed by Him in front of Moses. One of these signs involved changing Moses' staff into a serpent and then returning it to its original form (Exod. 4:2–5). The next sign consisted of making Moses' hand "leprous like snow," then restoring it "like the rest of his flesh" (vv. 6–7). The third sign would be performed if the people refused to accept the other two miracles. This supernatural act was going to involve turning some water from the Nile River into blood (vv. 8–9). In short, the Lord was promising Moses that he could count on His power to back up his words. That would surely give Moses all of the respect he required.

E. **Excuse Number Three: "I do not have all of the ability."** Moses was not finished resisting God's will. He retorted, " 'Please, Lord, I have never been eloquent, neither recently nor in time past, nor since Thou hast spoken to Thy servant; for I am slow of speech and slow of tongue' " (v. 10). Actually, Moses had been a powerful public speaker in Egypt (Acts 7:22b). But his forty years in the desert had not given him the opportunities needed to maintain that talent. Consequently, Moses felt inadequate to carry out the task God was calling him to.

F. **Answer Number Three: "But you will have all that is needed."** The Lord's response to Moses was direct and therapeutic: " 'Who has made man's mouth? Or who makes him dumb or deaf, or seeing or blind? Is it not I, the Lord? Now then go, and I, even I, will be with your mouth, and teach you what you are to say' " (Exod. 4:11–12). Moses did not need a refresher course in oratory skills. All Moses needed was to trust in God's ability and promise to supplement his weaknesses with divine strength.

G. **Excuse Number Four: "I am not as qualified as everyone else."** The New International Version captures Moses' thoughts well: " 'O Lord, please send someone else to do it' " (v. 13).† The bottom line was that Moses did not want to go back to Egypt. He was apparently not convinced that he had the prerequisites needed to accomplish the mission of deliverance. He felt inferior and incapable.

H. **Answer Number Four: "But you are My choice . . . however, I will send another person along with you."** Moses' final excuse brought the Lord to the end of His patience. With anger burning against him, God accommodated Moses' desire in part. That is, He commissioned Aaron, Moses' brother, to be the spokesman for Moses (vv. 14–16). Moses did choose to take Aaron along as God had permitted. But later, Moses regretted that decision.

III. God Sends Moses.

Moses finally returned to "Jethro his father-in-law" (v. 18a). But instead of telling him about the mission he had received from God, Moses said, " 'Please, let me go, that I may return to my brethren who are in Egypt, and see if they are still alive' " (v. 18b). Moses did not talk straight with Jethro. But he did receive Jethro's blessing (v. 18c). Once everyone's good-byes had been said, the Lord sent Moses off to Egypt (v. 19).

IV. Our Response to God.

We can resist God's will or we can submit ourselves to it. The choice is ours. But once we begin heeding His call, our acceptance needs to be marked by three traits.

A. **Certainty That It Is God's Voice.** We must be as sure as possible that we are listening to God and not simply trying to fulfill some personal desire that may be unbiblical or immoral. We may discern a great deal about God's will for our lives by coming to an accurate understanding of the Scriptures. For His desire is that all Christians conform their lives to His revealed standard. Anything that we believe to be God's will should be screened through the Bible. If it is inconsistent with Scripture, then it should not be regarded as the Lord's desire for our lives.

†*New International Version* (International Bible Society, 1978); cited from *The Comparative Study Bible: A Parallel Bible* (Grand Rapids: The Zondervan Corporation, 1984).

B. Confidence in God's Power. Once we conclude that the call is God's, we must rest in His power, not our own. We are never sufficient to handle His tasks, but He always is.

C. Comfort with His Plan. We should not resist His call or try to alter His plan. If we do, then we may find ourselves working out His arrangement with an "Aaron" by our side. It is far better when we refuse to compromise and we agree to receive what God gives, lack what He withholds, relinquish what He takes, suffer what He inflicts, and become what He requires.

🌺 *Living Insights*

Study One ▬▬▬▬▬▬▬▬▬▬▬▬▬▬▬▬▬▬

Isn't it incredible that we can read in the pages of our Bible a dialogue between a mere man and the God of the universe? Maybe their conversation has sparked some questions in your mind. If so, that's a good sign!

- The following chart provides an outline of an important skill in personal Bible study—*questioning*. It is when we ask questions of the text that we are on the road to the right answers. Use a copy of this chart as your guide through Exodus 3:10–4:19. As you ask the questions listed below, look for the answers in the text itself.

Exodus 3:10–4:19	
Questions	Answers
Who?	
What?	
Where?	
When?	
Why?	
How?	

🌸 Living Insights

"Who me, Lord?" Have you ever asked that question? Most of us probably have. Let's talk about this whole matter of *resistance*. Gather together a group of friends or, if possible, your family. The only rules for this *discussion* are that everyone should get to talk and all contributions should be accepted lovingly.

- How do you demonstrate resistance to God?
- How important is it to you to have all the answers?
- How do you handle feelings raised by the fear of not having the respect of others?
- What qualifies a person to be effectively used of God?
- What are some ways to be certain you are hearing God's voice?
- How do you appropriate God's power in your life?
- Why should we be comfortable with God's plan?

God's Will, God's Way
Exodus 4:18–31

It took God's persistent answers to convince Moses that He could use a failure to lead His people out of Egypt. And once Moses was certain that the only acceptable answer he could give was "Yes, Lord, I will go," he resisted no longer. Moses submitted to God's will and determined to carry it out God's way. As we shall see, he learned, through even the initial stages of his obedience, the truths conveyed in these two proverbs:

Trust in the Lord with all your heart,
And do not lean on your own understanding.
In all your ways acknowledge Him,
And He will make your paths straight.
(Prov. 3:5–6)
When a man's ways are pleasing to the Lord,
He makes even his enemies to be at peace
with him. (Prov. 16:7)

I.   Moses' Explanation to Jethro.

After Moses had all of his excuses addressed by God, he left the burning bush at Mount Sinai and returned to his home. He approached Jethro, his father-in-law and employer, with this request: " 'Please, let me go, that I may return to my brethren who are in Egypt, and see if they are still alive' " (Exod. 4:18a). Certainly, Moses was concerned about his fellow Hebrews. But by failing to mention his encounter with God, he possibly displayed some lingering doubts concerning how people might accept his mission. In any case, Jethro responded positively to Moses' request by telling Moses to depart with his blessing (v. 18b). Before Moses left, the Lord spoke these comforting words to him: " 'Go back to Egypt, for all the men who were seeking your life are dead' " (v. 19). Perhaps Moses' greatest underlying concern was that his return to Egypt would jeopardize his life. After all, he had fled the country once before because the king of Egypt had tried to kill him for murdering an Egyptian taskmaster (Exod. 2:12, 15). But the Lord reassured him that there was no longer anyone living in Egypt who sought to take his life.

> **Some Contemporary Application**
>
> Although Moses did not tell Jethro the real reason for his return trip to Egypt, he did the right thing when he went to his family before embarking on his journey. Similarly, once God crystalizes His calling in our lives, we should seek to tenderly sever any ties that we need to. Even though it is not always possible, we should attempt to gain the blessing of close family and friends before setting out on our divinely appointed tasks. This section of

Scripture also teaches us that when we are in the center of God's will, things flow. He begins to straighten out our crooked paths and starts to replace our anxieties with His perfect peace.

II. Moses' Trip to Egypt.

The text tells us that "Moses took his wife and his sons and mounted them on a donkey, and he returned to the land of Egypt. Moses also took the staff of God in his hand" (Exod. 4:20). Moses' shepherding staff had become God's because He had used it to perform a miracle and was planning to use it for many more later on (vv. 2–5, 17). Either before or during the journey, the Lord reiterated to Moses that he was to perform all the miracles he had been empowered to do. " 'But,' " the Lord added, " 'I will harden [Pharaoh's] heart so that he will not let the people go' " (v. 21). The Lord instructed Moses to follow His hardening activity with these words to Pharaoh: " ' "Thus says the Lord, 'Israel is My son, My first-born. So I said to you, "Let My son go, that he may serve Me"; but you have refused to let him go. Behold, I will kill your son, your first-born' " ' " (vv. 22–23). We will discover that this event preceded the tenth plague, where the firstborn of every Egyptian family died as the result of divine judgment on Pharaoh's disobedience to God (Exod. 11:4–10, 12:29–30). This miracle of devastation also may have been a delayed yet appropriate judgment from God for Egypt's policy of murdering all of the Hebrew male newborns (cf. Exod. 1:15–22). Now while Moses was on the road from Midian to Egypt, God sought to kill him, perhaps by causing him to become gravely ill (Exod. 4:24). The reason for this act of divine discipline concerned Moses' disobedience in not circumcising one of his sons (cf. Gen. 17:9–14). So his wife, Zipporah, circumcised the boy and threw his foreskin at Moses' feet (Exod. 4:25). Apparently, this act led to Moses' recovery (v. 26a) as well as the return of his family to Jethro's home in Midian (cf. Exod. 18:2–3).

Some Contemporary Application

There are at least four lessons for us in these verses. First, *when we are walking in God's desired will, whatever we use in the process becomes His property.* Our hands, voices, typewriters, computers, books, or any other instruments we might use become like Moses' staff—sacred tools in the hands of the living God. Second, *when we are doing God's will His way, we can perform even the most difficult assignment with a quiet confidence* (cf. Isa. 32:17). Moses the Hebrew was given the dangerous task of appearing before the Egyptian king and demanding that his largest work force be permitted to leave the country. When Moses heard God give him this command, he did not argue but simply listened and obeyed. He knew that the Lord would see him through, and that gave him the security he needed to carry it out. Third, *when we make the decision to trust God rather than ourselves, we will often find Him unearthing areas of our lives that we have neglected.* This occurred with Moses when he failed to obey the law of circumcision in God's covenant to the Hebrews. The Lord wants His chosen vessels to submit to Him in every aspect of their lives. Partial obedience will never do. Fourth, *God will often use those who are closest to us to expose the areas of our lives that need spiritual cleansing.* Zipporah was the instrument God used in Moses' life. We should be vulnerable to and even seek after the constructive observations of our mates, relatives, and friends. They will often help us become aware of blind spots that may be hindering our walk with God.

III. Moses' Encounter with Aaron.

When Moses began traveling alone to Egypt, the Lord sent Aaron, his brother, to meet him in the desert. Aaron found him "at the mountain of God"—that is, Mount Sinai. When he greeted Moses, "he kissed him" (Exod. 4:27). Then Moses proceeded to tell Aaron "all the words of the Lord with which He had sent him, and all the signs that He had commanded him to do" (v. 28). This marks the first recorded incident where Moses told someone about the revelation he had received from God through the burning bush.

Some Contemporary Application

Aaron was more than a blood brother to Moses; he was also a close friend. Moses could share his deepest secrets with him, knowing that they would fall on understanding and appreciative ears. We all need at least one person in our lives to whom we can relate intimately. The Lord knows this, and He is in the process of bringing us together. While we wait, we need to do what we can to be a good friend to others who cross our paths.

IV. Moses' Initial Experience with the Hebrews.

After Moses and Aaron arrived in Egypt, they "assembled all the elders of the sons of Israel." Then "Aaron spoke all the words which the Lord had spoken to Moses. He [Moses] then performed the signs in the sight of the people" (vv. 29–30). The event that followed occurred exactly as the Lord had predicted: "The people believed; and when they heard that the Lord was concerned about the sons of Israel and that He had seen their affliction, then they bowed low and worshiped" (v. 31).

Some Contemporary Application

The same people who had once refused to follow Moses' lead now believed that he was God's instrument of deliverance. The difference was that now Moses was doing God's will God's way, not his way. We can experience similar results in our lives if we will only choose to trust in God and refuse to lean on our self-made crutches.

🦁 *Living Insights*

The main thrust of our study can be summarized in a single statement: When you trust in the Lord *completely*, He'll guide your paths. This is succinctly communicated in Proverbs 3:5–6. These two verses open the door to the riches of that great book.

- The following chart lists some references from Proverbs on trusting God. Use it as a springboard for a topical study on this grand theme.

Results of Trusting God	
References	Results
Proverbs	
1:7	
2:5	
3:5–6	
4:4	
5:1–2	
6:23	
7:1–2	
8:13	
9:9–10	
10:27	
11:30	
12:21	
13:13	
14:26–27	
15:33	
16:3, 7, 20	

Living Insights

At the root of our relationship with God is that key concept—*trust.* It's been a central theme throughout Church history. A glance at a hymnal will underscore that fact.

- Locate a hymnbook. Flip through its pages, taking note of many of the instances where trusting in God is the message. Start with some of these hymns.
    - —"Only Trust Him"
    - —" 'Tis So Sweet to Trust in Jesus"
    - —"Trust and Obey"
    - —"Trusting Jesus"

If you feel like *singing them,* go ahead! If not, use the lyrics as a reminder of the importance God places on our trust.

Digging Deeper

One of the most controversial and misunderstood events in the Bible is the hardening of Pharaoh's heart. For many people, the incident demonstrates that man is simply a puppet in the hands of God. Other individuals have argued that this occurrence does not preclude human freedom, but it does show that God can and will override man's decisions on certain occasions. Still others have claimed that the event displays the compatibility of man's will and God's, while many people have thrown up their hands trying to understand the relationship between Pharaoh's activity and the Lord's. Regardless of the view one accepts, much can be learned about this happening through a careful study of the biblical text. We have taken the liberty to provide below a word study on the Hebrew terms used for *harden* and a chart that contains an orderly arrangement of the crucial data concerning Pharaoh's hardening. Following the chart, you will also find a brief list of resources that deal with the issues involved in the relationship between divine sovereignty and human freedom. If you decide to plummet the depths of this inexhaustible topic, you should discover this material to be an extremely helpful guide.

- **Definition of *Harden*.**
    Three different Hebrew words are translated "hardened" in relationship to Pharaoh's refusal to let the Israelites leave Egypt. The most frequently used word is *ḥāzaq* (Exod. 4:21; 7:13, 22; 8:19; 9:12, 35; 10:20, 27; 11:10; 14:4, 8, 17). It means "to make strong, to strengthen, to harden." The next most commonly used term is *kābēd* (Exod. 7:14, here translated "stubborn"; 8:15, 32; 9:7, 34; 10:1), and it expresses "dullness or insensitivity." The third Hebrew word

44

is *qāshâ* (Exod. 7:3), and it may be defined as "stubborn, stiff-necked." When considered together and in their specific contexts, these words express the same truth; namely, that Pharaoh was made more tenacious in his chosen path of unwillingness to allow the Hebrew people to leave Egypt. As the chart displays, sometimes Pharaoh confirmed himself in his established course of action, while on other occasions, God gave him the added courage to continue in his stubbornness. In either case, the terms do not exclude Pharaoh's exercise of freedom. Indeed, the words and their contexts presuppose that Pharaoh was already on a self-determined path of resistance before any hardening of his heart began to take place (cf. Exod. 5, where it is recorded that Pharaoh steadfastly refused to let the Hebrews go, and yet the text omits any mention that the hardening process predicted by God had begun).

● **Chart on Pharaoh's Hardening.**

The Hardening of Pharaoh's Heart—Exodus 4–14			
References	The Hardening Agent	The Time of the Hardening	The Purpose of the Hardening
4:21–23	Prediction of God as the agent	Prediction given before Moses arrives in Egypt; it refers to the hardening which occurs before the tenth plague	To confirm Pharaoh in his refusal to let the Hebrews leave
7:3–5	Prediction of God as the agent	Prediction given prior to Aaron's staff consuming the staffs of the Egyptians	To provide an opportunity for God to multiply His miracles of judgment so that the Egyptians will know that He is the Lord (cf. 9:13–17, 14:18)
7:13–14	Pharaoh	Just after Aaron's staff consumes the staffs of the Egyptians	None stated
7:22–23	Pharaoh	Just after the Nile River is turned to blood—the first plague	None stated
8:15	Pharaoh	Just after the frogs cover Egypt and die— the second plague	None stated

Continued on next page

45

References	The Hardening Agent	The Time of the Hardening	The Purpose of the Hardening
8:19	Pharaoh	Just after the gnats cover Egypt— the third plague	None stated
8:32	Pharaoh	Just after swarms of insects afflict the Egyptians and then die—the fourth plague	None stated
9:7	Pharaoh	Just after the livestock of the Egyptians die— the fifth plague	None stated
9:12	God	Just after boils break out on the Egyptians— the sixth plague	None stated
9:34–35	Pharaoh	Just after hail strikes Egypt and ceases— the seventh plague	None stated
10:1–2	God	A general statement about God's activity made prior to the plague of locusts	To multiply His miracles among the Egyptians so that future generations of Hebrews will know that He is the Lord (cf. 14:30–31)
10:20	God	Just after the locusts cover Egypt and die— the eighth plague	None stated
10:27	God	Just after darkness covers Egypt for three days—the ninth plague	None stated
11:9–10	God	A general statement about God's activity made prior to the death of the Egyptian firstborns	To multiply His miracles in Egypt
14:4–8	God	After the Hebrews begin to leave Egypt with Pharaoh's permission	To demonstrate to the Egyptians that God is the Lord

- **Sources on God's Sovereignty and Man's Freedom.**
Anselm, Saint. *Trinity, Incarnation, and Redemption: Theological Treatises.* Rev. ed. Edited and translated by Jasper Hopkins and Herbert W. Richardson. New York: Harper Torchbooks, 1970.

Berkouwer, G. C. *The Providence of God.* Translated by Lewis Smedes. Studies in Dogmatics. Grand Rapids: William B. Eerdmans Publishing Co., 1952.

Forster, Roger T., and Marston, V. Paul. *God's Strategy in Human History.* Foreword by F. F. Bruce. Wheaton: Tyndale House Publishers, Inc., 1973.

Geisler, Norman L. "Freedom, Free Will, and Determinism." In *Evangelical Dictionary of Theology.* Edited by Walter A. Elwell. Grand Rapids: Baker Book House, 1984.

Geisler, Norman L. "God, Evil, and Dispensations." In *Walvoord: A Tribute.* Edited by Donald K. Campbell. Chicago: Moody Press, 1982.

Geisler, Norman L. "Man's Destiny: Free or Forced?" *Christian Scholar's Review* 9:2 (1979), pp. 99–109.

Packer, J. I. *Evangelism and the Sovereignty of God.* Downers Grove: InterVarsity Press, 1961.

Pinnock, Clark H., ed. *Grace Unlimited.* Minneapolis: Bethany Fellowship, Inc., 1975.

Thiessen, Henry C. *Lectures in Systematic Theology.* Revised by Vernon D. Doerksen. Grand Rapids: William B. Eerdmans Publishing Co., 1979.

Yohn, Rick. *Living Securely in an Unstable World: God's Solution to Man's Dilemma.* Portland: Multnomah Press, 1985.

Going from Bad to Worse
Exodus 5–6

Most likely, we have all had days that began well, turned bad, and then became even worse. Moses had the same experience when he initiated his divinely appointed mission in Egypt. Soon after riding on the crest of an encouraging wave, Moses and Aaron were threatened by the reef of Pharaoh's resistance and dashed on the rocks of the Hebrews' resentment. Bruised and broken, Moses turned to God for His healing counsel. What he learned through this up-and-down experience provides us with timeless principles for handling our periods of deep discouragement.

I. **Pharaoh's Response to Moses** (Exodus 5:1–21).
    In this section of the narrative, a cycle of events is repeated three times. Each cycle is composed of an announcement, some reactions, expressed anger, and unjust blame. Let's follow the plot of the story as it unfolds.

    A. **Cycle One** (vv. 1–9). Following an uplifting spiritual conference with the Hebrew elders in Egypt (Exod. 4:29–31), Moses and Aaron appeared before Pharaoh with this demand: " 'Thus says the Lord, the God of Israel, "Let My people go that they may celebrate a feast to Me in the wilderness" ' " (Exod. 5:1). But the king of Egypt refused to fulfill the demand of a God he did not know (v. 2). So Moses and Aaron softened the demand by putting it in the form of a request (v. 3; cf. Exod. 3:18). But with great anger, Pharaoh again refused to grant their petition. And this time, he exposed his real motive for not permitting the Hebrews to leave—namely, that he was afraid he would lose his largest labor force (Exod. 5:4–5). So with blame on his lips, he issued a directive that greatly increased the work load of the Hebrews. Notice what the text says about this order:

    > So the same day Pharaoh commanded the taskmasters over the people and their foremen, saying, "You are no longer to give the people straw to make brick as previously; let them go and gather straw for themselves. But the quota of bricks which they were making previously, you shall impose on them; you are not to reduce any of it. Because they are lazy, therefore they cry out, 'Let us go and sacrifice to our God.' Let the labor be heavier on the men, and let them work at it that they may pay no attention to false words." (vv. 6–9)

    B. **Cycle Two** (vv. 10–14). The taskmasters and foremen carried out the new command they had been given. They announced it to the Hebrew workers, who obediently responded and tried their best to meet it (vv. 10–12). The taskmasters, however, began to push them harder, ordering them to complete their daily quota of bricks even though they now had to gather their own straw (v. 13). And when the Hebrews were unable to fulfill their quota under the new condition, the Egyptian taskmasters beat the Hebrew foremen and blamed them for their peoples' failure (v. 14).

C. **Cycle Three** (vv. 15–21). At this juncture, the anger of those involved began to intensify. The Hebrew foremen came before Pharaoh and appealed to him to renege on his decision (vv. 15–16). But he accused them of being lazy and commanded them to return to work without altering his command one bit (vv. 17–18). Then the foremen, realizing the impossibility of meeting his demand, went to Moses and Aaron and blamed them for their difficult situation. The text has preserved the harsh words the Hebrew foremen spoke to Moses and Aaron: " 'May the Lord look upon you and judge you, for you have made us odious in Pharaoh's sight and in the sight of his servants, to put a sword in their hand to kill us' " (v. 21).

II. **Moses' Response to God** (Exodus 5:22–6:1, 9, 12, 28–30). Here Moses was, finally doing God's will God's way. And what happened? Everything went wrong! Pharaoh rejected his request and tightened the screws of oppression on the Hebrews. Even Moses' people turned against him, faulting him for their increased labors. What do you think Moses did? He turned to the Lord and asked Him two familiar questions. Let's look at each one.

A. **"Why?"** Moses put the question in these words: " 'O Lord, why hast Thou brought harm to this people? Why didst Thou ever send me? Ever since I came to Pharaoh to speak in Thy name, he has done harm to this people; and Thou hast not delivered Thy people at all' " (Exod. 5:22–23). Although Moses had been warned by God that matters would go from bad to worse before they would get better (Exod. 3:19–22), he did not understand why the Lord was working out His plan in this way. Perhaps Moses thought that God had made a mistake in choosing him for the task. But God responded to Moses with a promise of action: " 'Now you shall see what I will do to Pharaoh; for under compulsion he shall let them go, and under compulsion he shall drive them out of his land' " (Exod. 6:1). With these fresh words of hope in his mind, Moses returned to the Hebrews and gave them the message that he had received from the Lord. "But they did not listen to Moses on account of their despondency and cruel bondage" (v. 9).

B. **"How?"** This further act of rejection sent Moses back to the Lord in prayer. But this time, his question was different:

" 'Behold, the sons of Israel have not listened to me; how then will Pharaoh listen to me, for I am unskilled in speech?' " (v. 12). Moses blamed his lack of eloquence for his failure to rally the Hebrews. And he concluded that if he could not persuade his own people to listen to him, then certainly Pharaoh would not heed his words (cf. vv. 28–30). Moses was definitely wallowing in the pits of despair.

III. **God's Response to Moses** (Exodus 6:2–8, 10–11, 13–29). The Lord did not leave Moses in an emotional lurch. He consoled and counseled Moses by reminding him about some truths regarding His nature and His will.

A. **"I Am."** Five times God said to Moses, " 'I am the Lord [*YHWH*]' " (vv. 2, 6, 7, 8, 29). By repeating this statement, the Lord was emphasizing Moses' need to stay focused on Him. What was true then is also true now. We will remain unable to endure those times that go from bad to worse until we rivet our attention on the Lord (cf. Heb. 12:1–3). We need to contemplate such characteristics as His sovereignty, goodness, power, justice, compassion, love, and wisdom—especially when we find ourselves sinking in treacherous waters. Because of who God is, we can be confident that He is in control of our circumstances.

B. **"I will."** Seven times the Lord addressed Moses' need by zeroing in on how He would intervene in his situation. Here are the promises He made to Moses:

" 'I will bring you out from under the burdens of the Egyptians, and I will deliver you from their bondage. I will also redeem you with an outstretched arm and with great judgments. Then I will take you for My people, and I will be your God. . . . And I will bring you to the land which I swore to give to Abraham, Isaac, and Jacob, and I will give it to you for a possession.' " (Exod. 6:6b–7a, 8a)

We can summarize God's message to Moses in these words: "Because I am who I am, I will always do what is best for you." If we would only believe this during those days that spiral downward, we would begin to see a marked change in our ability to handle them. God expected Moses to accept this truth as well and to get back to his appointed mission (vv. 10–11).

IV. **Our Response to Difficult Circumstances.** As we can see from this period in Moses' life, God does not want us to retreat when we are doing His will. The desire of our Lord is that we stand fast on His nature and His promises, looking to Him for strength and victory. And we will be able to do this more effectively when we recall the truths that are embedded in these verses of

Scripture. Each principle teaches us that tough times are designed by God for our good, not for our detriment.

A. Circumstances that turn against us force dependence.

B. Circumstances that force dependence teach us patience.

C. Circumstances that teach us patience make us wise.

 Living Insights

Study One ━━━━━━━━━━━━━━━━━━━━━━━━━━━━━━

Exodus 5–6 revolve around three major personalities: Pharaoh, Moses, and *YHWH.* Let's analyze their character traits.

• Copy the following chart into your notebook. As you read Exodus 5–6, look carefully for character descriptions of these three personalities and record them in the appropriate columns below.

The Main Personalities—Exodus 5–6					
Pharaoh		Moses		*YHWH*	
Verses	Character Traits	Verses	Character Traits	Verses	Character Traits

 Living Insights

Study Two ━━━━━━━━━━━━━━━━━━━━━━━━━━━━━━

Because God is who He is, He will do what is best for us. Even when things go from bad to worse, God provides a way for them to work for our benefit.

• Meditate on James 1:2–8. Try to get ahold of *The New Testament in Modern English,* by J. B. Phillips; it would be an outstanding version to use. Pay close attention to how God employs struggles as character builders in your life. This is an excellent passage to commit to memory if you've never done so. And remember, there is one key to meditation—*don't hurry.* Take small bites of God's Word and savor them slowly.

51

Plagues That Preach
Exodus 7–10

God is not a doting grandfather who treats disobedient children with a soft touch. He is the King of the universe. And when He speaks, He expects His subjects to sit up, listen, and obey. If they stubbornly refuse, then they risk becoming objects of His wrath. This fact is graphically illustrated in Exodus 7–10. Because Pharaoh elected to rebel against the divine King, he opened the door for ten destructive expressions of God's fury. Certainly this is a dark section of Scripture. However, the truths it conveys can bring even the most determined rebel to the light of God's mercy.

I. **Facts to Remember.**
Before we briefly examine the plagues delivered by God, we should recall three central facts.
   A. **God predicted the plagues.** The Lord told Moses from the burning bush that because of Pharaoh's refusal to release the Hebrews, He would strike Egypt with a series of miracles (Exod. 3:19–20). These acts of judgment were not afterthoughts; they were a part of the Lord's plan before Moses ever returned to Egypt.
   B. **Pharaoh's nature required the plagues.** As God had prophesied, Pharaoh rejected the Lord's command to permit the Hebrews to worship Him in the wilderness (Exod. 5:1–2). In fact, just prior to the start of the first plague, God said to Moses, " 'Pharaoh's heart is stubborn; he refuses to let the people go' " (Exod. 7:14). Because of Pharaoh's deep-rooted rebellious nature, the Lord had to deliver some devastating wonders in order to get his attention. Furthermore, his staunch disobedience to God called for a severe judgment. The plagues served both purposes very well.
   C. **Moses' question prompted the plagues.** When the Lord commanded Moses to return to Pharaoh and again demand the release of the Hebrews, Moses said to Him, " 'Behold, I am unskilled in speech; how then will Pharaoh listen to me?' " (Exod. 6:29–30; cf. vv. 10–12). Soon after Moses posed this question, God began showering the plagues upon Egypt. Pharaoh finally heeded Moses' words by the end of the tenth plague. What an incredible answer to Moses' question!

II. **Plagues to Consider.**
From even a cursory reading of Exodus 7–10, we can make two general observations about the plagues. First, *each plague affected all of the Egyptians.* God's judgment was thorough. And second, *none of the plagues softened Pharaoh's heart.* Even though he finally did allow the Hebrews to leave after the tenth plague, the fact that he later pursued

them in order to bring them back demonstrates that he never did repent of his disobedience to God. With these thoughts in mind, let's turn our attention to the first nine plagues. The tenth one will be discussed in the next lesson.

A. Blood. The first plague was the turning of the Nile River as well as all the other water in Egypt into blood (Exod. 7:14–25). This miracle killed all the fish that inhabited the Egyptian waters and made it virtually impossible for the people to find fresh water to drink (vv. 18, 21, 24). But the seven-day period of devastation made no impact on Pharaoh's unwillingness to let the Hebrews leave his nation (vv. 22b–25).

B. Frogs. The next plague consisted of a swarm of frogs that came up out of the waters and covered the entire land of Egypt (Exod. 8:1–15). These animals even made their way into the bedrooms, beds, ovens, and kneading bowls of the Egyptians (v. 3). In response, Pharaoh told Moses and Aaron that he would release the Hebrews if their God would remove the frogs (vv. 8–9). But once the Lord caused the frogs to die "out of the houses, the courts, and the fields," Pharaoh "hardened his heart" and reneged on his promise (vv. 13, 15).

C. Gnats. Unlike the first two plagues that were preceded by a warning, the plague of gnats came unannounced to Pharaoh (8:16–19). The Hebrew word translated "gnats" or "lice" was used to name a tiny, black insect that would penetrate the nostrils and ears of its victims and sting them. We are told that these insects covered man and beast "through all the land of Egypt" (v. 17b). When the Egyptian magicians could not duplicate this miracle, they exclaimed to Pharaoh, " 'This is the finger of God' " (v. 19a). "But," the text adds, "Pharaoh's heart was hardened, and he did not listen to them" (v. 19b).

D. Insects. In response to Pharaoh's continued belligerence, the Lord caused "great swarms of insects" to enter "the house of Pharaoh and the houses of his servants" (v. 24a). As they spread throughout "all the land of Egypt," they laid it to waste (v. 24b). The only area that was protected from the insects was the land of Goshen—the habitation of the Hebrews. To this plague Pharaoh reacted immediately, promising Moses and Aaron that he would permit the Hebrews to worship God if they would not travel very far into the wilderness (v. 28). Moses responded by asking the Lord to remove the insects from the land (vv. 29–30). However, after God answered Moses' request, "Pharaoh hardened his heart . . . , and he did not let the people go" (vv. 31–32).

E. Livestock Epidemic. The fifth plague was brought about through a " 'very severe pestilence' " that struck and killed all of the Egyptians' livestock without harming any of the Hebrews' animals (Exod. 9:3, 6). But, as had happened before, the judgment produced no change in Pharaoh's will. He again hardened his heart and refused to allow the Hebrew people to leave the Egyptian borders (v. 7).

F. Boils. The sixth plague, like the third one, came without warning. When Moses "took silt from a kiln" and "threw it toward the sky, . . . it became boils breaking out with sores on man and beast" (9:10). Even the Egyptian magicians were afflicted by these painful boils (v. 11). And for the very first time, we are told that *"the Lord* hardened Pharaoh's heart" (v. 12, emphasis added).

G. Hail. With Egypt's fish and meat supply already demolished, God turned His attention to the crops and vegetation that filled the land. He sent the worst hailstorm on Egypt that had ever been witnessed "since it became a nation" (9:24). We read that "the hail struck all that was in the field through all the land of Egypt, both man and beast; the hail also struck every plant of the field and shattered every tree of the field" (v. 25). Only the land of Goshen escaped the vicious hailstorm (v. 26). This plague prompted at least a momentary "repentance" and another promise of release from Pharaoh (vv. 27–28). But once the hailstorm ceased, the Egyptian ruler "sinned again and hardened his heart" (v. 34). Yet another time he reneged on his word to let the Hebrews go.

H. Locusts. Once again, "Moses and Aaron went to Pharaoh and said to him, 'Thus says the Lord, the God of the Hebrews, "How long will you refuse to humble yourself before Me? Let My people go, that they may serve Me" ' " (Exod. 10:3). But Pharaoh turned his face once more against the Lord. Consequently, God caused a huge number of locusts to cover "the surface of the whole land" (vv. 13–15a). There were so many of them that they darkened the entire Egyptian landscape and "ate every plant of the land and all the fruit of the trees that the hail had left. Thus nothing green was left on tree or plant of the field through all the land of Egypt" (v. 15). Again Pharaoh confessed his sin (vv. 16–17). But when the locusts were removed from Egyptian soil, "the Lord hardened Pharaoh's heart, and he did not let the sons of Israel go" (vv. 19–20).

I. Darkness. Then, again without warning Pharaoh, the Lord used Moses to bring about a "thick darkness in all the land of Egypt for three days" (10:22). The darkness was so great that the Egyptians could not "see one another, nor did anyone rise from his place for three days" (v. 23a). However, "all the sons of Israel had light in their dwellings" (v. 23b). In response to this oppressive plague, Pharaoh told Moses, " 'Go, serve the Lord; only let your flocks and your herds be detained. Even your little ones may go with you'" (v. 24). But when Moses told Pharaoh that he must release the Israelites *and* their livestock, "the Lord hardened Pharaoh's heart" so that he was once again unwilling to permit their departure (vv. 25–27). At this time, Pharaoh delivered his most stringent words to Moses: "'Get away from me! Beware, do not see my face again, for in the day you see my face you shall die!'" (v. 28). But Moses stood before him unafraid. With authority in his voice, he told the king of Egypt, "'You are right; I shall never see your face again!'" (v. 29). As we will see in our next lesson, the final plague God brought upon Egypt secured the release of the Hebrews.

III. Truths to Ponder.

This account of divine judgment has not been recorded and preserved simply for the sake of history. Events such as these have been written for our instruction in godly living (cf. 1 Cor. 10:1–11). So as we contemplate this account in Exodus, two life-changing thoughts stand out. Let's personalize them.

A. **When God judges, He does a thorough job.** If you have not placed your trust in Jesus Christ as your Savior—if you are still hardening your heart against Him—then you are under the wrath of God. As much as He desires to cleanse you from all wrongdoing, He cannot allow you to go unpunished for your sins. Don't wait for His judgment to fall. Today is the day of salvation. On the other hand, if you are a Christian, then do not take God's grace lightly. Because His love is so great, He will not permit us to continue in an ungodly lifestyle without disciplining us (cf. Heb. 12:5–11). So seek His face and repent of your disobedience. When you do, He will forgive and restore you (1 John 1:6–9).

B. **When God blesses, He holds nothing back.** While Egypt was receiving the brunt of God's wrath, Israel was reveling in the blessings of His grace. If you will just step out of the darkness of sin and set foot in the light of His mercy, then He will give you the abundance of His love both now and forever.

The Plagues of God and the Gods of Egypt
Exodus 7–12

Plagues	Warnings	Extent
1. Water turned to blood (7:14–25)	Given to Pharaoh (7:15–18, 20a)	"All the land of Egypt" (7:21b)
2. Frogs (8:1–15)	Given to Pharaoh (8:1–4)	"Covered the land of Egypt" (8:6b)
3. Gnats (or mosquitoes) (8:16–19)	None given	"All the land of Egypt" (8:17b)
4. Insects (or flies) (8:20–32)	Given to Pharaoh (8:20–23)	"All the land of Egypt" (8:24b)
5. Livestock epidemic (9:1–7)	Given to Pharaoh (9:1–5)	"All the livestock of Egypt died" (9:6b)
6. Boils (9:8–12)	None given	" 'On man and beast through all the land of Egypt' " (9:9b)
7. Hailstorm (9:13–35)	Given to Pharaoh (9:13–21)	"All the land of Egypt" (9:25a)
8. Locusts (10:1–20)	Given to Pharaoh (10:1–6)	"All the land of Egypt" (10:14a)
9. Darkness (10:21–29)	None given	"All the land of Egypt" (10:22b)
10. Death of the firstborns (11:1–12:32)	Given to Pharaoh (11:4–8)	"All the first-born in the land of Egypt" (12:29a)

Sources: The material on Egyptian deities given in this chart was drawn from John D. Hannah, "Exodus," in *The Bible Knowledge Commentary,* ed. by John F. Walvoord and Roy B. Zuck (Wheaton: Victor Books, 1985), p. 120; John H. Walton's *Chronological and Background Charts of the Old Testament,* foreword by Merrill C. Tenney, Academie Books (Grand Rapids: Zondervan Publishing House, 1978), p. 43; and John J. Davis' *Moses and the Gods of Egypt: Studies in the Book of Exodus* (Grand Rapids: Baker Book House, 1971), pp. 79–152.

Pharaoh's Responses	Possible Egyptian Deities Attacked by the Plagues
Hardened his heart, refused to listen, displayed indifference (7:22b–23)	Hapi—god of the Nile Isis—goddess of the Nile Khnum—guardian of the Nile
Dealt deceitfully, hardened his heart, refused to listen (8:8, 15)	Heqet—goddess of birth, with a frog head
Hardened his heart, refused to listen (8:19b)	Set—god of the desert
Dealt deceitfully, hardened his heart, refused to release the Hebrews (8:25–29, 32)	Re—a sun god Uatchit—a god possibly represented by the fly
Hardened his heart, refused to release the Hebrews (9:7b)	Hathor—goddess with a cow head Apis—the bull god, symbol of fertility Mnevis—sacred bull of Heliopolis
God hardened his heart, refused to listen (9:12)	Sekhmet—goddess with power over disease Sunu—the pestilence god Isis—goddess of healing
Dealt deceitfully, hardened his heart, refused to release the Hebrews (9:27–29, 34–35)	Nut—a sky goddess Osiris—god of crops and fertility Set—god of storms Seth—protector of crops
Dealt deceitfully, God hardened his heart, refused to release the Hebrews (10:16–17, 20)	Nut—a sky goddess Osiris—god of crops and fertility Seth—protector of crops
Proposed a bargain, God hardened his heart, refused to release the Hebrews, told Moses to leave (10:24–28)	Re, Aten, Atum, Horus—all sun gods Nut, Hathor—sky goddesses
Told Moses and Aaron to lead the Hebrews with their possessions out of Egypt (12:31–32)	Min—god of reproduction Isis—goddess who protected children Heqet—goddess of birth Pharaoh's firstborn son—a god

🌿 *Living Insights*

Our God is a God of order. Even in the midst of these terrible plagues, there is a *pattern* to His work. Let's put into practice a creative method of viewing His consistency.

- This exercise will necessitate the use of six different-colored pencils or pens. As you read through Exodus 7–12, *color code* the words in these chapters that correspond to the divisions given below. Circle or underline the appropriate words with the color of your choice in each of the ten plagues. You should soon begin to observe similar patterns of color in this passage. Here's the breakdown.

Divisions	Suggested Colors
God Speaking	Blue
Moses Speaking	Green
Pharaoh Responding	Red
The Plagues	Purple
The Effects of the Plagues	Orange
The References to the Israelites	Brown

🌿 *Living Insights*

The studies we've conducted thus far have caused us to interact with such topics as failure, self-discovery, resistance, and insecurity. Let's turn the tables and reflect on the final application made in this study: When God blesses, He holds nothing back!

- The hymn writer says to "count your blessings; name them one by one." Have you made a list like that lately? Take some time to reflect on God's past and present blessings in your life. As they come to mind, write them out and thank the Father for giving them to you.

The Night Nobody Slept
Exodus 11–12

We have seen that God touched the Egyptians with nine severe strokes of judgment. We have also noticed that after each one, Pharaoh stubbornly refused to permit the Hebrews to depart from his nation. In this study, however, we will witness the preparations for and the arrival of the tenth catastrophe—the final blow aimed at Pharaoh's hardened heart. It is with devastating finality that the almighty Lord deals the knockout punch to the king of Egypt and delivers His people from slavery. As we recount this event, we will discover afresh that doing God's will God's way demands both our availability and our obedience.

I. The Prediction: A Plague of Sorrow.

After God had caused thick darkness to cover Egypt for three days, Pharaoh once again rejected Moses' demand to release the Hebrew people along with their possessions (Exod. 10:21–27). Pharaoh's repeated disobedience to the Lord finally led to the last and most tragic plague.

A. Announced to Moses. The Lord told Moses the basics of His plan and the part the Hebrews were to play in it:

"One more plague I will bring on Pharaoh and on Egypt; after that he will let you go from here. When he lets you go, he will surely drive you out from here completely. Speak now in the hearing of the people that each man ask from his neighbor and each woman from her neighbor for articles of silver and articles of gold." (Exod. 11:1–2)

The command for the people to take articles of silver and gold when they left was an odd one. But later, the Hebrews would understand that the reason for securing these items was for the building of a tabernacle in the wilderness of Sinai.

B. Received by Israel. Verse 3 goes on to tell us that "the Lord gave the [Hebrew] people favor in the sight of the Egyptians." In addition, Moses became "greatly esteemed ... both in the sight of Pharaoh's servants and in the sight of the people." No longer was Moses looked down upon and ignored. The Lord had brought him respect, even before his enemies (cf. Prov. 16:7).

C. Heard and Rejected by Pharaoh. Moses went to the Egyptian ruler and pronounced divine judgment upon him and his people. He told Pharaoh that " 'all the first-born in the land of Egypt' " would die at midnight (Exod. 11:4–5). He added that this act would cause great sorrow in all the homes of Egypt. The homes of the Israelites, however, would be spared because the Lord had promised that the plague would not harm them

(vv. 6–7). In fact, the end result would be the release of the Hebrew people. Once Moses gave this prophecy, he left Pharaoh's presence "in hot anger" (v. 8). Then the Lord spoke to Moses again and said, " 'Pharaoh will not listen to you, so that My wonders will be multiplied in the land of Egypt' " (v. 9). The stage was almost set for the Hebrews' bondage to end. There was only one more preparation that had to be made.

II. The Memorial: The Passover Meal.

The Lord spoke to Moses and Aaron, informing them that they needed to prepare the Israelites for the plague which was soon to occur. He instructed the Hebrews to establish an ordinance—a memorial meal that would mark the first month of every subsequent year for them (Exod. 12:2, 14). Let's consider the details of this observance and discover why the Lord wanted them to perform it.

A. **Some Details to Observe.** The basics of the meal were simple. Each Hebrew household, or group of households, was to choose one lamb on the tenth day of the first month (12:3–4). The lambs were to be unblemished, one-year-old males (v. 5a). On the fourteenth day of the same month, all of the Israelites were to kill these special lambs at the twilight hour (v. 6). Some of the blood that spilled from the carcasses was to be put on the two doorposts and lintels of each Israelite home where the meal was going to be eaten (v. 7). That same evening the lamb was to be roasted and completely consumed, with unleavened bread and bitter herbs as the side dishes (vv. 8–10). The Hebrews were to hastily eat this meal with their loins girded, their sandals on, and their staffs in hand (v. 11). Why were they commanded to do all these things? Verses 12–13 make the reason clear:
" 'For I will go through the land of Egypt on that night, and will strike down all the first-born in the land of Egypt, both man and beast; and against all the gods of Egypt I will execute judgments—I am the Lord. And the blood shall be a sign for you on the houses where you live; and when I see the blood I will pass over you, and no plague will befall you to destroy you when I strike the land of Egypt.' "

B. **An Event to Remember.** This Passover rite was not only to be observed in Egypt, but also after the Hebrews reached the Promised Land. One reason God wanted it established as a "permanent ordinance" was so that the Israelite children would never forget what the Lord had done for their ancestors in Egypt (vv. 14, 24–27a).

C. **The Response of the Hebrews.** When the Israelites heard what the Lord wanted them to do and why, they "bowed low and worshiped" Him (v. 27b). Then they went and did all that "the Lord had commanded Moses and Aaron" (v. 28). Now that they knew and understood God's will for them, they responded in obedience.

III. The Fulfillment: Death of the Firstborns.

When the midnight hour struck, God did exactly what He said He would. The Lord killed "all the first-born in the land of Egypt, from the first-born of Pharaoh who sat on his throne to the first-born of the captive who was in the dungeon, and all the first-born of cattle" (v. 29). Once Pharaoh and the other Egyptians realized what had happened, "a great cry" arose, "for there was no [Egyptian] home where there was not someone dead" (v. 30). In response to this devastation, Pharaoh "called for Moses and Aaron at night and said, 'Rise up, get out from among my people, both you and the sons of Israel; and go, worship the Lord, as you have said. Take both your flocks and your herds, as you have said, and go, and bless me also'" (vv. 31–32).

IV. The Exodus: Freedom for the Hebrews.

This final plague launched the mass exit of the Israelites from the borders of Egypt. The text tells us that the Lord delivered them on the very day that marked "the end of [their] four hundred and thirty years" in Egypt (v. 41a). This lengthy period probably came to an end in 1445 B.C.* As the Hebrews departed, they requested and received "from the Egyptians articles of silver and articles of gold, and clothing," just as the Lord had commanded them (vv. 35–36). We are told that the Israelites "journeyed from Rameses to Succoth" and that they numbered "about six hundred thousand men on foot, aside from children" (v. 37). Accompanying them was a "mixed multitude" of possibly other Semites and some native Egyptians as well as their flocks, herds, and other livestock (v. 38). Psalm 105 adds that God "brought forth His people with joy" (v. 43a). Certainly this was an incredible event that only the Lord of lords could have possibly accomplished!

> **A Historical Note**
> Although we are not given an exact count, many Bible scholars estimate that the number of men, women, and children who left in the Exodus was over two million. John J. Davis provides the

---

*For some excellent discussions on this question, see *Moses and the Gods of Egypt: Studies in the Book of Exodus,* by John J. Davis (Grand Rapids: Baker Book House, 1971), pp. 148–50; and *A Survey of Old Testament Introduction,* by Gleason L. Archer, Jr. (Chicago: Moody Press, rev. ed., 1974), pp. 223–34.

> reasoning behind this conclusion: "The number of men over twenty years of age is listed as 600,000. . . . Assuming that males over twenty constitute approximately one-fourth the population, the total number of Israelites involved in the exodus would have surpassed 2,000,000 people."†

V. Your Life: Slavery or Freedom?

If you have not been born into God's everlasting family, then you are like Israel was in Egypt—a victim of oppression. The only way you can be freed from the shackles that bind you is to trust in Jesus Christ for the forgiveness of your sins. If you are a child of God, then you need to respond obediently to His will as revealed in Scripture. For freedom from the power of sin is found in obedience to divine truth. As Jesus said, " 'If you abide in My word, then you are truly disciples of Mine; and you shall know the truth, and the truth shall make you free' " (John 8:31b–32). Furthermore, if you stand before God as a disciple of His Son, then you need to make yourself available to His special call in your life. The Israelites were willing and ready to move from the familiar to the unfamiliar at the moment God told them to go. We should be just as prepared to change locations, jobs, or even careers if the Lord calls on us to do so. Are you ready? Will you be obedient when He calls?

---

†John J. Davis, *Moses and the Gods of Egypt: Studies in the Book of Exodus* (Grand Rapids: Baker Book House, 1971), p. 146.

🌹 Living Insights

Exodus 11 and 12 provide another snapshot in the biography of Moses. A careful look will reveal that this chapter in his life really has four subheadings. Without referring to the lesson, try to capsulize this part of his story by completing the following exercises:

• Write a summary of the details that occurred during the plague recorded in Exodus 11:1–10.
• Paraphrase the details of the Passover meal as they are spelled out in Exodus 12:1–28.
• Recount the fulfillment of God's plan revealed in Exodus 12:29–36.
• Express your thoughts concerning the freedom the Israelites experienced as described in Exodus 12:37–42.

🌹 Living Insights

Isn't it exciting to see the way God worked in the life of Moses? In no uncertain terms, this man was God's choice to lead God's people. How well do you identify with Moses? Let's do a little assessment of your current ministry in the lives of others. Take a few minutes to copy and complete the chart given below.

An Assessment of My Current Ministry
In what tangible ways am I presently serving the Lord by ministering to people?
What are the strengths in my current ministry?
What are the weaknesses in my current ministry?
How can I minister more effectively in the next six months?

Between the Devil
and the Deep Red Sea
Exodus 14

People use such expressions as "in a pinch," "in a pickle," "in a jam," "up a tree," "in a corner," "hard-pressed," or "between a rock and a hard place" to describe a predicament. But whatever the expression, the meaning is the same—someone is facing a troubling situation that cannot be easily escaped. These dilemmas are uncomfortable and nerve-racking. They often bring us to the end of our resources and threaten to drive us into despair. An ancient illustration of just such a predicament is found in Exodus 14. There we will discover how the Hebrews were rescued from a humanly impossible situation that involved the pursuing Egyptians. This documented miracle will provide four lessons that we need to apply to our "Red Sea" experiences.

I. The Red Sea Miracle.

The two million or more Hebrews who were leaving Egypt had probably picked up Egyptian habits, styles, and even moral standards. But God wanted His people to be different. His desire was that they conform to a lifestyle that reflected His standard of righteousness. So He began their training with clear manifestations of His presence, power, and sovereignty. For example, He led them toward the eastern border of Egypt by "going before them in a pillar of cloud by day . . . , and in a pillar of fire by night" (Exod. 13:21a). In this way, everyone in the Israelite camp would know that the Lord was their ever-present Guide.

A. The Lord's Plan.
Even though God was directing the Hebrews, His plan was not to lead them to safety—at least not right away. His design was to place them in a predicament that was impossible to escape without His intervention. The Lord initiated His plan by having Moses " 'tell the sons of Israel to turn back [from Etham] and camp before Pi-hahiroth, between Migdol and the sea' " (Exod. 14:2a; cf. 13:20). Once they arrived there, they were to " 'camp in front of Baal-zephon, opposite it, by the sea' " (14:2b). At this location they would be just south of several massive Egyptian fortresses, north of the barren Egyptian desert, west of the deep Red Sea,* and east of the approaching Egyptian

---

*The Hebrew term *yam sûph* is often translated "Red Sea" (Exod. 13:18). Many contemporary Bible scholars understand the word to mean "the Sea of Reeds," while others question this opinion. But regardless of its meaning, the central issue is which body of water the word refers to. Unfortunately, no consensus has been reached on this question. Suffice it to say, however, that the water must have been deep enough to drown at once a large number of Egyptian soldiers. For more details on the identification of the "Red Sea," see *Moses and the*

army. In other words, God led His people into a geographic cul-de-sac—the most vulnerable spot they could be in militarily.

B. The Egyptians' Pursuit. With the Hebrews on their way toward the Egyptian border, it did not take long for Pharaoh and his servants to have "a change of heart" (v. 5). Pharaoh set out after the Israelites, taking with him "six hundred select chariots, and all the other chariots of Egypt with officers over all of them" (vv. 6–7). This formidable army became visible to the Hebrew camp as it rose over the Egyptian horizon with the dust from its horses and chariots billowing into the sky.

C. The Hebrews' Panic. The sight of the approaching Egyptian army evoked fear in the hearts of the Hebrews (v. 10a). Their first response was to cry out to the Lord (v. 10b). Their second reaction was to blame Moses for their quandary. Notice the stinging and ungrateful words that they spoke:

> "Is it because there were no graves in Egypt that you have taken us away to die in the wilderness? Why have you dealt with us in this way, bringing us out of Egypt? Is this not the word that we spoke to you in Egypt, saying, 'Leave us alone that we may serve the Egyptians'? For it would have been better for us to serve the Egyptians than to die in the wilderness." (vv. 11–12)

In response to their panic, Moses gave specific instructions coupled with timely counsel. He told them not to fear the advancing Egyptians and to " 'stand by and see the salvation of the Lord' " (v. 13a). For soon the Hebrews would witness how mightily the Lord would fight in their behalf while they silently looked on (v. 14). Indeed, the devastation caused by the Lord would be so complete that the Hebrews would never see these Egyptian soldiers again (v. 13b).

D. The Lord's Protection. With Pharaoh's military in hot pursuit of the Israelites, the Lord enacted a plan that would culminate in both protection for His people and judgment on the Egyptians. First, He commanded Moses to move the Israelites toward the sea (vv. 15–16). Second, "the angel of God, who had been going before the camp of Israel, moved and went behind them; and the pillar of cloud moved from before them and stood behind them" (v. 19). By doing this, the Lord blocked the children

---

Gods of Egypt: Studies in the Book of Exodus, by John J. Davis (Grand Rapids: Baker Book House, 1971), pp. 168–71; *A Survey of Israel's History,* by Leon Wood (Grand Rapids: Zondervan Publishing House, 1970), pp. 129–30; and "Exodus, The," by John Rea, in the *Wycliffe Bible Encyclopedia,* 2 vols., edited by Charles F. Pfeiffer, Howard F. Vos, and John Rea (Chicago: Moody Press, 1975), pp. 571–72.

of Israel from the Egyptians' view. This kept the advancing army from catching up to the Hebrews (v. 20). It also prevented the Hebrews from seeing the Egyptians so that their fear would not paralyze them. Third, God miraculously created a path of escape through the Red Sea. The account tells us that "Moses stretched out his hand over the sea; and the Lord swept the sea back by a strong east wind all night, and turned the sea into dry land, so the waters were divided" (v. 21). Once the passageway was dry, the Israelites "went through the midst of the sea on the dry land, and the waters were like a wall to them on their right hand and on their left" (v. 22). When the Egyptians saw the Hebrews making an escape, they resumed the pursuit by chasing them "into the midst of the sea" (v. 23). As the army drew closer, the Lord set the fourth step of His plan in motion: "He caused their chariot wheels to swerve, and He made them drive with difficulty; so the Egyptians said, 'Let us flee from Israel, for the Lord is fighting for them against the Egyptians'" (v. 25). What happened next marks the greatest event of deliverance in Old Testament history:

> Then the Lord said to Moses, "Stretch out your hand over the sea so that the waters may come back over the Egyptians, over their chariots and their horsemen." So Moses stretched out his hand over the sea, and the sea returned to its normal state at daybreak, while the Egyptians were fleeing right into it; then the Lord overthrew the Egyptians in the midst of the sea. And the waters returned and covered the chariots and the horsemen, even Pharaoh's entire army that had gone into the sea after them; not even one of them remained. (vv. 26–28)

E. The Hebrews' Praise. It must have been an incredible sight to see the Egyptians retreating into the water as it was collapsing on them. And the sight of Egyptian bodies and armaments washing onto the shore must have left the Hebrews awestruck by God's power. In fact, the text records that when they witnessed this supernatural event, they "feared the Lord, and they believed in the Lord and in His servant Moses" (vv. 30b–31).

II. Our "Red Sea" Experiences.

This account of a remarkable event in the history of Israel was not recorded simply for our amazement. But like all of the Old Testament Scriptures, it "was written for our instruction, that through perseverance and the encouragement of the Scriptures we might have hope" (Rom. 15:4b). Given this fact, there are four timeless lessons suggested in Exodus 14 that we would be wise to remember when our backs are up against a humanly impregnable wall.

A. **It takes tight places to break lifetime habits.** Some of our sinful thoughts, words, or actions have become so entrenched that we need to be placed in a spiritual cul-de-sac where we must face and deal with them.

B. **When hemmed in on all sides, the only place to look is up.** It's amazing how times of intense pressure can help us look beyond ourselves and put our trust in God. Situations such as these tend to reduce our selfishness and increase our teachability.

C. **If the Lord is to get the glory, then He must do the fighting.** When we hit those threatening impasses, we often panic and try to run. However, there is a better approach. We might state it like this: "When I wait, He fights; when He fights, He wins; when He wins, I learn." The only sure way to honor God and grow through a predicament is to turn the situation over to Him. Once you do, stay out of His way and watch Him work.

D. **"Red Seas" open and close at the Lord's command, not until.** God is not tied to our time schedules. He *will* deliver us from those circumstances that threaten to crush us, but not before we have learned the lessons that He wants to teach us.

Living Insights

Study One

"On the horns of a dilemma," "driven to the wall," "behind the eight ball," "in a squeeze"—no matter how you say it, there's no tougher spot than being in a dilemma without a human answer!

- After copying the following chart into your notebook, go back over Exodus 14. Observe what Moses did *right* and what the children of Israel did *wrong*. As you do, write down some *principles for passing through predicaments*. Try to find at least eight of them.

Principles for Passing through Predicaments	
Principles	References

Living Insights

Old Testament experiences have modern-day lessons. They pass on timeless truths from which we can learn. The four applications of this lesson are listed below. Following each one are some questions intended to stimulate your thinking. Answer them honestly, reflecting on how God uses those difficult situations in your life to mold you into His image.

- It takes tight places to break lifetime habits.
    —Have there been some tight places in your life?
    —What habits were broken as a result?
- When hemmed in on all sides, the only place to look is up.
    —When were you hemmed in on all sides?
    —What new qualities did God mold into your life?
- If the Lord is to get the glory, then He must do the fighting.
    —Why do we tend to take our battles into our own hands?
    —How has God become victorious in your life apart from you?
- "Red Seas" open and close at the Lord's command, not until.
    —When have you questioned God's timing in your life?
    —What lessons did you learn as a result of His timing?

A Heavenly Diet vs. an Earthly Appetite

Exodus 15:1–17:7

We have all had to take tests sometime during our lives. Whether they have been in school, at tryouts or auditions, on the job, or for securing a driver's license, tests are nearly impossible to escape. And it's no different in our vertical relationship with God. The Lord takes us through wilderness experiences for the purpose of refining our characters and driving us to trust in Him. Although these spiritual exams are often trying, they are essential to our growth in righteousness. This truth is clearly illustrated in the desert trials of the Hebrew people. And as we will see, the way they responded to the tests God gave is all too similar to the way we usually react in such situations. So let's drop our guards and open our hearts to the lessons we are about to learn. Only in doing so will we be prepared to pass our spiritual tests with flying colors.

I. The Geographical Setting.

Before we consider some of the exams God gave to the Hebrews, let's get our bearings geographically. In our last study, we saw how the Lord miraculously delivered the Israelites from the pursuing Egyptian army. We also observed how once their foe had been destroyed, the Hebrews "feared the Lord, and they believed in the Lord and in His servant Moses" (Exod. 14:31b). The text goes on to add that the people expressed their gratitude to God by singing to Him a song of praise (Exod. 15:1–18). Even "Miriam the prophetess, Aaron's sister, took the timbrel in her hand, and all the women went out after her with timbrels and with dancing. And Miriam answered them, 'Sing to the Lord, for He is highly exalted; / The horse and his rider He has hurled into the sea'" (15:20–21). What a day of rejoicing this was for God's people! But their time of praise on the east bank of the Red Sea did not last long. We are told that "Moses led Israel from the Red Sea, and they went out into the wilderness of Shur" (v. 22a). The Desert of Shur was in the northern section of the Sinai Peninsula. It stretched from the eastern border of Egypt to the southern edge of Palestine and probably reached as far south as the mountains of the Sinai Peninsula. Even today, this area is largely devoid of vegetation, except in places around springs and wells.* It was into this territory that the Lord led Israel. In fact, the Hebrews spent forty years wandering in barren deserts like Shur. Why? Deuteronomy 8:2 tells us: "'And you shall remember all the way which the Lord your God has led you in the wilderness these forty years, [so] that He might humble you, testing you, to know what

---

*John J. Davis, *Moses and the Gods of Egypt: Studies in the Book of Exodus* (Grand Rapids: Baker Book House, 1971), pp. 176–77.

was in your heart, whether you would keep His commandments or not.' " In other words, their desert experience was designed to stretch and exercise their spiritual muscles so that they would grow in their obedience to and dependence on God.

II. The General Cycle.

While the Israelites were sojourning in the wilderness, their responses to God's tests often followed a pattern that we still repeat today. Let's take a quick glance at each step in this cycle.

   A. **Abundance from God.** The Hebrews experienced the fruitful blessing of God when they were saved from the Egyptian army by His miraculous power (Exod. 14:21–31). This event led to their songs of thanksgiving (Exod. 15:1–21).

   B. **Expectations of More.** The tangible fruit of God's blessing usually leads to the expectation that more is still to come. It's not difficult to imagine that the Hebrews had the same expectation when they left the banks of the Red Sea for the Desert of Shur.

   C. **Disappointments with Less.** When expectations are not met, disappointments arise. This certainly occurred among the Hebrews when they traveled three days into the desert region of Shur and found no drinkable water (15:22–23).

   D. **Complaints over Circumstances.** Disappointments over unmet expectations often bring complaints. Israel fulfilled this segment of the cycle when she "grumbled at Moses" over her water situation (v. 24).

   E. **Provision from God.** Fortunately for believers, the Lord often responds to our complaints with answers of provision. He did this for the Hebrews after Moses cried out to Him in prayer, for we read that God caused the bitter waters to become sweet (v. 25a). Then He spoke the following words to the people of Israel: " 'If you will give earnest heed to the voice of the Lord your God, and do what is right in His sight, and give ear to His commandments, and keep all His statutes, I will put none of the diseases on you which I have put on the Egyptians; for I, the Lord, am your healer' " (v. 26). The principle God gave was clear: "Obey Me, and I will surround you with My protective arms." As we will see, this involved satisfying the need, not the greed, of His people.

III. The Actual Circumstances.

With this general information about the cycle in mind, let's examine three specific tests that God gave to Israel.

   A. **The Time Test.** The first exam was given after the Lord had led His people to Elim. There they camped beside the "twelve springs of water and seventy date palms" (15:27). Then He led them "out from Elim, and . . . to the wilderness of Sin, which is between Elim and Sinai." This occurred 1½ months after their miraculous departure "from the land of Egypt" (Exod. 16:1). The Israelites' move from the abundance of Elim into the barrenness of Sin led to their complaining against Moses and Aaron (v. 2). After only a short period of time, the Hebrews were already disregarding the mighty ways God had met their needs.

B. The Hunger Test. After miserably failing the time test, the Hebrews set themselves up for the hunger exam. They did this when they spoke these words of complaint to Moses and Aaron: " 'Would that we had died by the Lord's hand in the land of Egypt, when we sat by the pots of meat, when we ate bread to the full; for you have brought us out into this wilderness to kill this whole assembly with hunger' "(v. 3). This shows that they conveniently focused on the few benefits they had in Egypt while completely ignoring the many sufferings that had been inflicted on them there. With this unjust complaint ringing in their ears, Moses and Aaron told the people that their grumblings were actually directed against God, not them (vv. 7b, 8b). They also assured the Israelites that the Lord had heard their complaints and would abundantly satisfy their hunger. And so He did, by supplying them with meat in the evening and bread every morning. Indeed, God gave them bread six days a week for the forty-year period they were in the desert (vv. 8–35). But even though they never went hungry, the Hebrews still managed to gripe about the lack of variety in the food God supplied for them. Notice the reason for their complaint: " 'We remember the fish which we used to eat free in Egypt, the cucumbers and the melons and the leeks and the onions and the garlic, but now our appetite is gone. There is nothing at all to look at except this manna' " (Num. 11:5–6). They had grown so accustomed to Egyptian cuisine that they regarded God's basic provision for their hunger with contempt. Their securely anchored habits led to their failure of another exam.

C. The Thirst Test. From the Desert of Sin, God led His people to Rephidim, which was just northwest of Mount Sinai. Once they reached this destination, the Hebrews discovered that there wasn't any water to drink (Exod. 17:1). So they "quarreled with Moses" and commanded him to give them water (v. 2). In fact, their demand became so intense that Moses cried out to God in fear for his life (v. 4). Once again, the Lord answered Moses' prayer and miraculously met the physical need of the Israelites in spite of their failure to pass another of His exams (vv. 5–7).

71

IV. Some Practical Conclusions.

Unfortunately, we can all see our reflections in the experiences of the Hebrews—that is, if we are honest with ourselves. Through careful meditation on these biblical accounts, three relevant lessons will surface that we all should apply.

A. It takes a humble attitude to learn from earthly tests. God doesn't want us to simply endure the tests He gives us. His desire is that we learn from them so that we will grow in Him. But this takes humility. Pride has no place in a teachable spirit.

B. It takes a heavy attack to break a daily habit. Nothing is more difficult to "unlearn" than ungodly habits. That is why God must assault them repeatedly until they are finally broken.

C. It takes a heavenly appetite to enjoy a heavenly diet. The natural response of an earth-centered appetite is grumbling. However, if our appetite is to accomplish God's will in His way, then the provisions He supplies will satisfy our needs.

Living Insights

There's a general cycle that often develops in wilderness experiences—abundance, expectations, disappointments, complaints, and provision. Let's move ahead a few decades to see another cycle that the children of Israel fell into.

● After Moses died, Joshua led the Israelites. When he departed, a group of leaders known as the *judges* took over. This was a dark period in the history of Israel. You can get a thumbnail sketch of this era by observing the cycle of the people recorded in Judges 3:7–11. The pattern then repeats itself in verses 12–15. See if you can discover the five steps of this cycle. As you do, record them in a copy of the following chart. If you have time, search out the other five occurrences of the cycle in Judges. The extra moments you spend will be worthwhile.

The Steps of the Cycle in Judges
1.
2.
3.
4.
5.

🐟 *Living Insights*

This passage addresses a key issue in our lives—*complaining*. Complaints are expressed in a variety of ways, but they all communicate our disappointments. Let's review this issue in the lives of the Israelites.

- Reread Exodus 15–17. Pay particular attention to the Hebrews' complaints. What were their gripes? How did Moses respond to them? How did God deal with them? What's the correlation between the Israelites' complaints and the Lord's activity? What lessons can be learned from these chapters that can help you in your life?

Why Leaders Crack Up
Exodus 18

Someone has said, "Good men die young." We could easily add to that
"...and most leaders crack up." Why is this true? Among the many reasons
we could give, one is predominant: Leaders have the tendency to do too
much and delegate too little. It's easy for leaders to become so saddled
with petty details and problems that they can't find enough time to
accomplish the essentials of their jobs. And when they try to compensate
by putting in more work time, they eventually become exhausted,
frustrated, angry, and lonely. Unfortunately, this is not a new problem.
Moses experienced it as he became submerged beneath the numerous
needs of the Israelites. Indeed, his burden grew to such proportions that
he was laboring "from the morning until the evening" every day
(Exod. 18:13). Does God provide any solutions to this draining problem?
He certainly does! And they can be unearthed from the rich soil of
Exodus 18. So let's examine this passage with the expectation that there
we will find some valuable answers to this practical problem of leadership.

I. A Visit from Jethro.
The miracle of the Exodus was now behind the Hebrews. Before them
lay Canaan—the abundant land of divine promise. However, between
Egypt and Canaan were many miles of desert and several tests of trust.
Early during their wilderness wanderings, Moses received an
unexpected visit from his father-in-law, Jethro. He brought with him
Moses' wife, Zipporah, and his two sons, Gershom and Eliezer
(Exod. 18:1–4). They met Moses at the Israelite camp, which was beside
Mount Sinai (v. 5). When Moses received word that they were coming,
he "went out to meet his father-in-law, and he bowed down and kissed
him; and they asked each other of their welfare, and went into the
tent" (vv. 6–7). But this joyful reunion did not end outside. Once inside
the tent, "Moses told his father-in-law all that the Lord had done to
Pharaoh and to the Egyptians for Israel's sake, all the hardship that
had befallen them on the journey, and how the Lord had delivered
them" (v. 8). To this great news, Jethro responded with reverent
gladness:

> And Jethro rejoiced over all the goodness which the Lord had
> done to Israel, in delivering them from the hand of the
> Egyptians. So Jethro said, "Blessed be the Lord who delivered
> you from the hand of the Egyptians and from the hand of
> Pharaoh, and who delivered the people from under the hand
> of the Egyptians. Now I know that the Lord is greater than all
> the gods; indeed, it was proven when they dealt proudly
> against the people." Then Jethro, Moses' father-in-law, took a
> burnt offering and sacrifices for God, and Aaron came with all

the elders of Israel to eat a meal with Moses' father-in-law before God. (vv. 9–12)

II. An Evaluation of Moses.

On the day following this wonderful time of celebration, Moses returned to what had become his tiresome duties.

A. Moses' Practice (vv. 13–16). Daily, "Moses sat to judge the people, and the people stood about Moses from the morning until the evening" (v. 13). When Jethro saw all the work and time that Moses was putting in, he asked him, " 'What is this thing that you are doing for the people? Why do you alone sit as judge and all the people stand about you from morning until evening?' " (v. 14). Jethro's first question concerned *priorities*. He did not understand why Moses' judging activity had been allowed to supplant his central task of leading God's people. The second question Jethro asked related to *personnel*. He failed to see why Moses alone was judging the people. To these queries, Moses supplied the following answer: " '[I alone judge the Hebrews] because the people come to me to inquire of God. When they have a dispute, it comes to me, and I judge between a man and his neighbor, and make known the statutes of God and His laws' " (vv. 15b–16).

B. Jethro's Correction (vv. 17–23). Once Moses answered, Jethro responded with decisiveness, insight, and honesty. The first thing he told Moses was that he was performing his job in a way that was detrimental to everyone involved. As he stated it to Moses, " 'You will surely wear out, both yourself and these people who are with you, for the task is too heavy for you; you cannot do it alone' " (v. 18). Moses already knew that his judging task was exhausting. What he needed was a solution; and Jethro gave it to him. His answer came in two wise pieces of advice.

1. **"You represent the people and teach them"** (vv. 19–20). The first bit of counsel Jethro gave was that Moses represent the people before God and that he instruct them in God's Word and way. By taking on these responsibilities, he could provide leadership for the whole group much better than he could when he was trying to address their needs individually.

2. **"You choose some qualified men to help you lead the people"** (v. 21–23). Jethro's second piece of direction was specific and clear: " 'Furthermore, you shall select out of all the people able men who fear God, men of truth, those who hate dishonest gain; and you shall place these over them, as leaders of thousands, of hundreds, of fifties and of tens. And let them judge the people at all times; and let

it be that every major dispute they will bring to you, but every minor dispute they themselves will judge. So it will be easier for you, and they will bear the burden with you'" (vv. 21–22). In other words, he was telling Moses to delegate his incidental responsibilities and to retain his essential ones. If Moses would follow his father-in-law's counsel, then he would be able to endure his job and the Israelites would find a greater degree of peace (v. 23).

III. A Change in Method.

Moses wisely chose to accept Jethro's advice. In fact, he enacted it to the letter. As the text records, "So Moses listened to his father-in-law, and did all that he had said" (v. 24; cf. vv. 25–26). Once Moses applied Jethro's method of leadership, "Moses bade his father-in-law farewell, and he went his way into his own land" (v. 27).

IV. Some Principles for Today.

This chapter in the life of Moses contains several valuable guidelines for people in any leadership position. Here are four of the prevailing principles for us today.

A. **In every responsibility, two factors are present—the essential and the additional.** The essentials of a leader's job are those matters that are crucial to accomplishing a given task. As such, they are obligations that a leader must perform. On the other hand, all other areas are additionals—that is, they are tasks that a leader may enjoy doing but that are not central to his or her leadership role. Therefore, they can, and in many cases should, be delegated to others. This brings us to the second principle.

B. **As the work load increases, the wise leader restrains his involvement and involves others more.** This principle is especially difficult to apply for those people who have held a leadership position in a company that has undergone great growth. Many times, such individuals continue to operate with a method of leadership that can only be effective in an environment where the work load is light. But when the responsibilities increase, a person must adapt his or her leadership style and recruit gifted, capable people to help carry the burden of the additional work load.

C. **God's servants are not exempt from the penalties of breaking life's natural laws.** Failure to delegate sufficiently will inevitably lead to a physical, emotional, or mental breakdown. No one can continue functioning under intense pressure and long working hours without cracking in some way. That is how God has designed us. He never meant for us to tackle a task that required more than one person to accomplish. So when we try to operate against His design for us, we are actually violating His laws, not keeping them as some might think.

D. Efficiency is increased not only by what is accomplished but also by what is relinquished. Whenever we believe that we can or should do it all and at the same time maintain a high standard of productivity and excellence, our minds should reflect long and hard on Moses' ineffective leadership methods. Not only did he exhaust himself, but he failed to meet the numerous needs of the Israelites. However, Moses' situation was remedied because he chose to apply some sound advice. And like Moses, only when we begin doing the essentials and delegating the incidentals will we experience both relief and success.

🦁 *Living Insights*

Study One ━━━━━━━━━━━━━━━━━━━━━━━━━━━━━━━━━━━━━━

Why do leaders crack up? Because they don't *delegate.* The wise leader knows that efficiency is increased by discerning essentials and being ready to relinquish other tasks to capable associates.

• Read Exodus 18 with the eyes of a wise leader. The following chart will help you discern the thrust of the teaching on delegation found in this passage. Copy the chart into your notebook; then begin your study, filling in the chart as you go.

Discerning Delegation—Exodus 18
Observations on Life without Delegation
Specifics on How to Delegate Properly
Results of Proper Delegation

🦁 Living Insights

Many of us suffer from the problem of superefficiency. We are so capable in a variety of tasks that we are unwilling to share the load with those around us. Are you a delegator? Let's seek an honest answer to that question.

- Are you ready to hear the straight facts about your efficiency? You may not be able to discern your own situation because you're too close to be objective. Thus, you need a "Jethro"—a man or woman of God who loves you and cares enough to tell you the truth about your life. Get together with a person like this and ask him or her to tell you both the strengths and the weaknesses of your approaches to leadership. This individual may praise you about areas of strength or may have to confront you about areas of weakness. But if you're prepared to respond honestly and humbly, this meeting could revolutionize your life!

Sinai: Where Moses Met God
Exodus 19–31

There are many instances recorded in Scripture where God spoke to His people. There are far fewer biblical accounts of the Lord actually appearing to believers. But most of the times that the Lord did manifest Himself to believers, the reaction He received from them was the same—reverential awe of His majesty and appropriate fear of His holiness. For example, Joshua "fell on his face to the earth, and bowed down" when he realized that he was conversing face-to-face with the Lord (Josh. 5:14). And Isaiah the prophet quaked with fear when he heard the holy God speak to him during a vision (Isa. 6:1–5). In this lesson we will climb Mount Sinai with Moses as he meets the great *YHWH* once again. As we will discover, this incredible account leaves no room for an anemic view of God or a halfhearted walk in His grace. Indeed, we will see that the righteous Lord of all commands that His people come to Him prepared to hear and obey. And thankfully, there are guidelines in this passage that will show us how we can prepare to meet Him on a regular basis. So let's gear up and join Moses for some climbs to the summit of the mountain of God.

I. Getting Ready for the Meeting (Exodus 19:1–15).
While Moses was shepherding Jethro's flock in Midian, the Lord told him that after the Exodus, he would come and worship Him at Mount Sinai. God explained to Moses that this would be a sign of His perpetual presence (Exod. 3:12). Three months after the Hebrews were delivered from their bondage in Egypt, "they came into the wilderness of Sinai" just as the Lord had promised (Exod. 19:1). After their arrival He began to prepare them for worship. God's plan involved two basic steps: leading them to the right place and requiring of them certain commitments. Let's consider both elements of His plan.

  A. The Specific Place (vv. 1–2). Generally, the location was the Desert of Sinai. Specifically, the spot was Mount Sinai—one of several granite mountains in this barren region. The text says that Israel set up camp in front of this huge mountain (19:2).

  B. The Specific Commitments (vv. 3–15). Once the two-million-plus Israelites were settled in, Moses made the arduous journey up the side of the mountain to meet with God. During his several encounters with the Lord, he received a list of requirements, all meant to prepare the Hebrews for their engagement with God.

   1. A Willingness to Obey. The Lord spoke to Moses and commanded him to convey these words to Israel: " ' "If you will indeed obey My voice and keep My covenant, then you shall be My own possession among all the peoples, for all the earth is Mine; and you shall be to Me a kingdom of priests and a holy nation" ' " (vv. 5–6a). When Moses descended the mountain and delivered this message to the elders, "the people answered together and said, 'All that the Lord has spoken we will do' " (vv. 7–8a). With this commitment made, Moses ascended the mountain and brought the people's response to the Lord (v. 8b).

2. **A Sensitivity to Hear.** Again the Lord spoke to Moses, saying, " 'Behold, I shall come to you in a thick cloud, in order that the people may hear when I speak with you, and may also believe in you forever' " (v. 9a). God wanted the Israelites to listen to His directives and trust His chosen leader, Moses. So He began to lay the appropriate groundwork for their receptivity.

3. **A Consecration of Heart.** After Moses communicated the second command to the Hebrew people, he climbed the mountain again and received another message from God: " 'Go to the people and consecrate them today and tomorrow, and let them wash their garments; and let them be ready for the third day, for on the third day the Lord will come down on Mount Sinai in the sight of all the people' " (vv. 10–11). In other words, the Israelites were to have clean clothes as well as unsoiled souls before coming to meet with God. Their outer cleanliness was to be a reflection of their inner purity.

4. **A Respect for God.** The final condition for worship that the Hebrews received was stated in these words: " 'And you shall set bounds for the people all around, saying, "Beware that you do not go up on the mountain or touch the border of it; whoever touches the mountain shall surely be put to death" ' " (v. 12). The Israelites' respect for the Lord was to be so deep that they would not even touch the place that marked His presence. *A Note of Application:* Too many of us have a shallow concept of God. As a consequence, we have an anemic walk with Him. The Lord is not a senile grandfather, a Hollywood superstar, or a neighborhood buddy. He is the Creator, Sustainer, Redeemer, and Judge of the entire universe. He deserves—indeed demands—our utmost reverence and ultimate obedience. And He expects nothing less.

II. The Meeting at the Mountain (Exodus 19:16–31:18).

After the Israelites had fulfilled all of the requirements God had given them, they awoke on the third day to a storm they would never forget (19:14–16). We read these words concerning this event:

There were thunder and lightning flashes and a thick cloud
upon the mountain and a very loud trumpet sound, so that
all the people who were in the camp trembled. And Moses
brought the people out of the camp to meet God, and they
stood at the foot of the mountain. Now Mount Sinai was all
in smoke because the Lord descended upon it in fire; and
its smoke ascended like the smoke of a furnace, and the
whole mountain quaked violently. When the sound of the
trumpet grew louder and louder, Moses spoke and God
answered him with thunder. (vv. 16b–19)

What an incredible sight this must have been! But why did the Lord
choose to reveal Himself to Moses and the Hebrews in such a
miraculous way? This section of Scripture gives us two reasons God
had for meeting with His people at Mount Sinai.

A. To Establish a Healthy Fear of the Almighty. As the
people stood trembling before this remarkable manifestation of
God's presence, they heard Moses speak these words: " 'Do not
be afraid; for God has come in order to test you, and in order
that the fear of Him may remain with you, so that you may not
sin' " (Exod. 20:20). A wholesome respect for the all-powerful
Judge is a marvelous deterrent to giving in to sin.

B. To Communicate Written Instructions for Israel. The
other reason God met with Israel was to reveal the Law and the
design of the tabernacle (Exod. 31:18, 25:8–9). Both sets of
instructions were given so that God's people would know how
to live righteously and worship appropriately in His eternal
presence.

III. Some Practical Guidelines for Today.

This portion of the Bible points out what should be the number one
priority in the life of every believer—*regular meetings with God.* What
we call them—whether it be devotions, quiet times, or communions
with God—is incidental. However, it is absolutely essential that we
have these times. Fortunately, these chapters provide us with several
guidelines that we can apply with great benefit to ourselves and our
relationship with Him. Let's briefly consider and personalize each one.

A. To meet regularly with God, you need a place. It may
be a room in your home, a spot in your office, or a place
outdoors. But whatever the location, it should be accessible,
private, quiet, and conducive to study and prayer.

B. To approach God, you need to be prepared. You should
never come to the Lord with an idle mind or a flippant attitude.
When you approach His throne, go with the willingness to obey,
the sensitivity to hear, the desire to be cleansed, and the attitude
of respect He deserves. Furthermore, you should plan to spend

quantitative, not just qualitative, time with the Lord. We would suggest a period of thirty minutes or more as usually sufficient for a meaningful meeting with God.

C. To hear from God, you need the Scriptures. The only written revelation we have from God is the Bible. Through it, He speaks with ringing relevance to every generation of believers. You need to take the time to read, study, and apply His infallible Word.

D. To remember what God says, you need a journal. This should be a record of your spiritual walk with God, not a diary of your daily activities. You might wish to write out some of your prayers, lessons you have learned from Scripture, or concerns about your relationships with both God and others. But whatever you include on a regular basis, use these words from Gordon MacDonald as a guide: "The main value of a journal is as a tool for listening to the quiet Voice that comes out of the garden of the private world. Journal keeping serves as a wonderful tool for withdrawing and communing with the Father."*

---

*Gordon MacDonald, *Ordering Your Private World* (Chicago: Moody Press, 1984), p. 146.

Living Insights

"And the Lord came down on Mount Sinai, to the top of the mountain; and the Lord called Moses to the top of the mountain, and Moses went up" (Exod. 19:20). What followed was the giving of the Law. This was certainly a momentous event in history!

● Let's imagine you're the ace reporter for the local newspaper *The Sinai Tribune.* Your editor has assigned you to do a story on the several meetings Moses had with God on the Law and other matters. Reread the Scriptures covered in the outline of this lesson and write a news article—headlines and all—about this incredible event. And don't forget the reporter's best friends—questions like *who, what, where, when, why,* and *how.*

Living Insights

In a very real sense, this study has to do with the most important priority of our lives. It is well worth the time to look more personally into *our meetings with God.* Let's use the four points of application from this lesson as a checklist for our personal times with the Lord.

● To meet regularly with God, you need a place.
—Where's your place?
—Is it suitable for studying, praying, and listening?
● To approach God, you need to be prepared.
—Do you go to Him with an active mind and a willing heart?
—Are you entering His presence with the attitudes of humility and respect?
● To hear from God, you need the Scriptures.
—Do you have a Bible that you're comfortable using?
—Do you use a variety of study methods?
● To remember what God says, you need a journal.
—Do you keep a spiritual journal?
—How can these "Living Insights" help you start or maintain a written record of your spiritual walk?

Particular Perils of the Godly
Numbers 10–14

After the Hebrews arrived at Mount Sinai, two major events occurred: God gave His Word to them in written form, and they constructed a portable tabernacle for the purpose of worshiping the Lord. With these two happenings in their memories, the Israelites began their journey toward Canaan—the land of divine promise. Moses encountered several perilous situations as he led the people under God's direction. And what he faced is not rare in the lives of the godly today. In this lesson we will gain an understanding of the risks that threatened Moses, and we will draw from them some timeless truths that can aid us in our exposure to spiritual hazards.

I. **Understanding the "Peril Principle."**
   Before we set our sights on Moses, let's take a few moments to get a grip on the peril principle and examine some of its occurrences in the Bible.
   A. **The Word *Peril* Defined.** In Webster's dictionary, the term *peril* means "exposure to the risk of being injured, destroyed, or lost."* In other words, a peril is not something that has occurred or will occur. Rather, a peril is the threat of something that *could* happen in a certain situation.
   B. **The Peril Principle Stated.** Spiritually speaking, the axiom is this: *Those who determine to walk with God become targets of the enemy.* Satan is not overly concerned with believers who merely play at Christianity. However, those believers who are committed to living consistently for Christ lay themselves open to demonic attacks that are meant to make them spiritually useless.
   C. **The Peril Principle in Scripture.** When we scan God's Word, we can find numerous passages that communicate and amplify this characteristic of the Christian life. Among these texts, three stand out above the rest.
      1. **Second Timothy 3:12.** This passage says that "all who desire to live godly in Christ Jesus will be persecuted." No measure of uncertainty is conveyed here. Anyone who decides to live righteously before God will suffer as a result.
      2. **First Peter 5:8–9.** Here Christians are commanded to "be on the alert" because their "adversary, the devil, prowls about like a roaring lion, seeking someone to devour." In this passage believers are also exhorted to resist Satan with a firm faith, "knowing that the same experiences of suffering

Webster's New Collegiate Dictionary (Springfield: G. & C. Merriam Co., 1979).

85

are being accomplished by [their] brethren who are in the world." Satan's attacks are not bound geographically. He seeks to assault every person who desires to become godly.

3. **Psalm 4:3.** In this verse we learn that "the Lord has set apart the godly man for Himself" and that He hears the prayers of such an individual. Put another way, when we choose to live for the Lord, He takes us under His protective wings and pays special attention to our petitions. Thus, we can rest assured that He is with us as we traverse the hazardous terrain of life.

II. A Case Study: Moses.

Moses was not only God's man for a crisis, but he was also God's man for perilous situations. Even though he did not always handle them as he should, he did confront them with the determination to consistently walk in God's ways. This is clearly illustrated in chapters 10–14 of Numbers. In this section of Scripture, we read that Israel had begun her second year in the desert (Num. 10:11). We are also told that the Lord had guided her out of "the wilderness of Sinai" and into "the wilderness of Paran"—a desert region which was northeast of Mount Sinai (v. 12). The Hebrews were on their way to Canaan. But their journey would not be void of risks—especially for Moses. Indeed, this account informs us about five perils Moses faced as Israel's leader. These hazards are still experienced by believers today.

A. **The Peril of Discouragement and Depression.** Moses had to deal with this potential trap while the Hebrews were settled in the Desert of Paran. The text records that "the people became like those who complain of adversity in the hearing of the Lord; and when the Lord heard it, His anger was kindled, and the fire of the Lord burned among them and consumed some of the outskirts of the camp" (Num. 11:1). As a result, the Israelites "cried out to Moses, and Moses prayed to the Lord, and the fire died out" (v. 2). However, the complaining did not stop.

> The rabble who were among them had greedy desires; and also the sons of Israel wept again and said, "Who will give us meat to eat? We remember the fish which we used to eat free in Egypt, the cucumbers and the melons and the leeks and the onions and the garlic, but now our appetite is gone. There is nothing at all to look at except this manna." (vv. 4–6)

When Moses witnessed the continued pettiness and ungratefulness of the people, he became displeased and discouraged. He turned to the Lord and asked Him the questions of a downhearted person (vv. 11–13). Moses' queries, along with his petition for God to kill him, reveal the intensity of his depression (v. 15). As we can see, Moses fell prey to a peril that is common to us all. But the Lord did not abandon him. He set a plan in motion that eventually lifted much of the burden that had weighed Moses down so severely (vv. 16–25).

B. **The Peril of Jealousy and Indispensability.** With the plan God had initiated came another spiritual hazard. Until this time, Moses had been the only prophet in the Israelite camp. But after God appointed seventy elders and empowered them to prophesy, Moses' position lost its unique status (vv. 24–25). This change did not bother anyone until two of the seventy elders remained in the Hebrew camp, prophesying as the Holy Spirit directed them (v. 26). This act prompted two men, one of whom was Joshua, to exhort Moses to " 'restrain them' " (vv. 27–28). Apparently, these two individuals perceived that Moses' position as leader and prophet was being threatened. But Moses did not become jealous or bolster himself up with feelings of indispensability. Instead, he said, " 'Would that all the Lord's people were prophets, that the Lord would put His Spirit upon them!' " (v. 29b). Moses understood that the Lord was the sovereign Head. Consequently, he could look upon God's activity in the lives of others with joy rather than jealousy.

C. **The Peril of Being Misunderstood and Misrepresented.** This trap was set for Moses by two of his family members, Aaron and Miriam, while they were camped in Hazeroth (Num. 11:35–12:1). They were upset by Moses' marriage to a "Cushite woman," which probably took place after Zipporah's death (Num. 12:1). There were no legal restrictions against Hebrews marrying Cushites (Exod. 34:11–16). However, Aaron and Miriam became envious over this union because they saw Moses' new wife as a threat to their positions of leadership among the Israelites (Num. 12:2). So the Lord rebuked their misunderstanding and misrepresentation of Moses and his wife, and He punished them by inflicting Miriam with leprosy for seven days (vv. 3–15). Moses did not have to defend himself against their slanderous charges. For the Lord came to his aid and effectively laid their accusations to rest.

D. **The Peril of Being Ignored and Rejected.** After the Israelites "moved out from Hazeroth and camped in the wilderness of Paran" again, Moses sent out several leaders into Canaan on a reconnaissance mission (Num. 12:16, 13:1–24). When they returned, all but Caleb and Joshua delivered a frightening report about the size and the fierceness of the land's inhabitants (Num. 13:25–33). As a result, "all the sons of Israel grumbled against Moses and Aaron" in fear for their lives (Num. 14:2–3). They even discussed appointing a new leader who would take them back to Egypt (v. 4). With these words of rejection ringing in their ears, "Moses and Aaron fell on their faces in the presence of all . . . the sons of Israel" (v. 5). Joshua and Caleb "tore their clothes" and pleaded with the people to stop their rebellion and seize the Promised Land (vv. 6–9). "But all the congregation said to stone them" (v. 10a). The Hebrew people had chosen to completely ignore and reject their counsel and leadership.

E. **The Peril of Resentment and Revenge.** The Israelites' abusive actions could have easily led Moses to retaliate. But he spurned this response and urged God to spare the people for His name's sake (vv. 11–19). The Lord answered Moses' plea by pardoning the Hebrews and disciplining them less severely. His judgment was that none of those who had left Egypt in the Exodus would be permitted to enter the Promised Land. The only exceptions to this directive were Caleb, Joshua, and those who had been born after the Exodus (vv. 20–35).

III. Some Practical Conclusions.

Moses managed to handle many of the hazards that he faced. We can have a solid track record with perils as well if we will recall these truths when threatened.

A. **The godly life is never easy.**
B. **The godly life is often endangered.**
C. **The godly life is always eventful.**

Living Insights

Those who determine to walk with God become targets of the enemy. This is so because commitment to the Lord brings with it certain perils. Consequently, we need to be prepared.

- With the help of a Bible concordance, let's do a word study on one particular peril. The hazard you choose should be the one with which you most personally identify. Write down your observations on a copy of the following chart. This exercise will provide you with some information that can help you overcome at least one spiritual hazard.

My Particular Peril	
Verses	Observations

 Living Insights

The particular perils of the godly can be devastating. They may not only affect the individual but also the whole Body of Christ.

- Spend a few minutes reflecting on the effects of these perils both in your life and in the Church. Then enter your thoughts on this pertinent subject in a copy of the chart below.

Particular Perils of the Godly		
Perils	Effects on Me	Effects on the Church
Discouragement		
Depression		
Jealousy		
Indispensability		
Being Misunderstood		
Being Misrepresented		
Being Ignored		
Being Rejected		
Resentment		
Revenge		

A Moment of Rage

Numbers 20:1–13

Down the street, a woman is brutally raped. Across town, three teenage boys and two elderly women lay on the street critically injured—victims of another gang war. The local television anchorman reports that the police have found three men dead and one fatally wounded. Apparently, the trouble had started over a disagreement that had arisen on the job. We can all recount stories such as these. Tragically, acts of violence in our society are not rare; they are even on the increase. And non-Christians are not the only guilty parties. For example, in Christian circles the number of wife and child abuse cases is beginning to escalate. You see, we all have the potential to strike out in a moment of rage and seriously, if not fatally, harm someone. Even Moses, the great Hebrew leader, had his fits of uncontrolled anger. How did God deal with these outbreaks? What do His dealings with Moses on this issue show us about how He may handle us when we behave in a similar manner? The answers to these questions and more are given in the lesson before us. Here we will discover how we can live in obedience rather than in rage.

I. The Matter of Anger.

Psychologists who have done in-depth studies on anger have concluded that there are five levels of intensity in this emotion. The first level of anger is *irritation*—a feeling of uneasiness that is brought about by an unpleasant disturbance. The second level is *indignation,* which is a reaction to something that is perceived to be unreasonable or unfair. The next stage is *wrath.* When this level is reached, it must be expressed in some way. For with wrath comes a strong desire to avenge or defend oneself. *Fury,* the fourth level of anger, usually manifests itself in acts of violence that are sometimes accompanied by a temporary loss of sanity. The fifth level is *rage,* and it is the most hostile and dangerous stage. Rage can overcome people to such a degree that they will explode with acts of brutality, devoid of any conscious awareness of their violent outbursts. This analysis of anger shows the practical need for us to control our tempers. But there is little hope of self-control if we do not have a saving relationship with Jesus Christ. For unbelievers lack what believers have—the Holy Spirit. He is the ever-present Regulator of a Christian's life. And only through His power can people receive the additional help they need to bring potentially harmful feelings of anger under control.

II. The Anger of Moses.

Unfortunately, believers do not always draw upon the restraining power of God. A case in point is Moses. Let's zero in on his tragic track record so that we might glean some timeless lessons that can help deter our anger as we rely on God's strength.

A. Past History. We can trace Moses' hostile flare-ups all the way back to his early adult years in Egypt. As we may recall, Moses was indignant when he witnessed an Egyptian beating a fellow Hebrew. His rage led to an act of fury that left the Egyptian murdered and Moses fleeing the country for his life (Exod. 2:11–15, Acts 7:23–29). The next recorded outbreak occurs about forty years later, after Moses had announced the coming of the tenth plague on all the Egyptian firstborns. The text informs us that "he went out from Pharaoh in hot anger" (Exod. 11:8b). Apparently, Moses was furious that Pharaoh had not allowed the Israelites to leave even though God had told him on several occasions that the Egyptian ruler would be extremely stubborn. Several months following this event, Moses again expressed his anger. We read that he descended Mount Sinai, carrying the Ten Commandments inscribed by God on two stone tablets. Once he was down the mountain, he saw the Israelites dancing around an idolatrous golden calf. This sight filled Moses with righteous indignation (Exod. 32:15–19a). What was wrong, however, was the way he chose to express his anger. The Scriptures tell us that "he threw the tablets from his hands and shattered them at the foot of the mountain. And he took the calf which they had made and burned it with fire, and ground it to powder, and scattered it over the surface of the water, and made the sons of Israel drink it" (vv. 19b–20). The text never adds that God condoned Moses' response of rage. Instead, a subtle condemnation of his anger occurs when the Lord commands him to take two more stone tablets and reinscribe the Ten Commandments onto them *himself* (Exod. 34:27–28).

B. Present Example. In Numbers 20:1–13, we are exposed to the last recorded eruption of Moses' hot temper. By this juncture, he has been leading the people of Israel for almost forty years in the desert region between Egypt and Canaan. Much of the time the Israelites have been complaining. As a result of this disobedience, the Lord has been killing those who had departed from Egypt in the Exodus. Among the exceptions to this divine act of judgment were Caleb, Joshua, and Moses. Finally, we read about their arrival to "the wilderness of Zin"—a desert area just south of the Promised Land (Num. 20:1). But as had happened on previous occasions, the people found no water to drink. So "they assembled themselves against Moses and Aaron" (v. 2). The complaint the Hebrews leveled against them had an all-too-common ring:

The people thus contended with Moses and spoke, saying, "If only we had perished when our brothers perished before the Lord! Why then have you brought the Lord's assembly into this wilderness, for us and our beasts to die here? And why have you made us come up from Egypt, to bring us in to this wretched place? It is not a place of grain or figs or vines or pomegranates, nor is there water to drink." (Num. 20:3–5)

This grievance sent Moses and Aaron to the Lord in prayer. God's answer to Moses was gracious and specific: " 'Take the rod; and you and your brother Aaron assemble the congregation and speak to the rock before their eyes, that it may yield its water. You shall thus bring forth water for them out of the rock and let the congregation and their beasts drink' " (v. 8). His directions were clear. Moses was not to do anything to the rock except speak to it. But once again, he openly disobeyed by allowing his anger to burst out of control. After the Israelites were gathered around the designated rock, Moses spoke these words of indignation: " 'Listen now, you rebels; shall we bring forth water for you out of this rock?' " (v. 10). Then he "lifted up his hand and struck the rock twice with his rod; and water came forth abundantly, and the congregation and their beasts drank" (v. 11). Although God still caused the miracle to occur, He sternly rebuked Moses and Aaron for violating His method of performing it. As He told them, " 'Because you have not believed Me, to treat Me as holy in the sight of the sons of Israel, therefore you shall not bring this assembly into the land which I have given them' " (v. 12). If Moses had only spoken to the rock, then this miracle would have pointed to the power of God. But he took it upon himself to angrily rebuke the Hebrews and, in a fit of rage, he struck the rock twice with his rod. By doing this, he turned the people's focus from the Lord and onto himself. It is clear that Moses failed one too many times, for the ultimate consequence was painful. Moses would not be allowed to lead the Hebrews into the land of divine promise.

III. Some Lessons to Learn.

It doesn't take much reflection on this tragic incident before we begin to see the many lessons that it teaches. However, if we focus our attention on God's words of rebuke to Moses in chapter 20, verse 12, then we can narrow down the essential lessons to these three. It should go without saying that our remembrance of them can help deter our anger from being expressed in ungodly ways.

A. An act of disobedience stems from unbelief (v. 12a).

B. A public act of disobedience diminishes God's glory (v. 12b).

C. An act of disobedience, though forgivable, can bear painful consequences (v. 12c).

 ## Living Insights

Study One

Numbers 20 records more than a momentary loss of self-control. As the first part of our study suggests, Moses wrestled with anger during most of his adult years. But for now, let's concentrate on his striking the rock in rage and on God's response to his outburst.

- Earlier in this study guide, you tried your hand at *paraphrasing*. Take up that Bible study method again by writing out Numbers 20:1–13 in your own words. Since this is definitely a feeling-filled passage, work at drawing the emotions out of the text as you encounter them. Feel Moses' anger, put yourself in the place of the Israelites, and attempt to identify with God's heart as He refused Moses' entrance into the Promised Land.

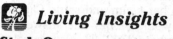 ## Living Insights

Study Two

We've carefully studied how Moses' uncontrolled anger decreased his effectiveness. Now, what about you? Since you're a member of the human race, you have to come to grips with keeping your anger in check. What steps have you taken to restrain its growth? Use the following chart to help you record your thoughts and some appropriate Bible references.

My Strategy for Controlling Anger	
Steps	Scriptures

Filling the Shoes of Moses
Numbers 27:12–23

Tears must have welled up in Moses' eyes when the Lord told him that he would not be allowed to enter the Promised Land. But piercing through his disappointment was the stark reality that Israel needed a suitable replacement—an individual who could help her claim and settle Canaan. How could the right person be found? Who would he be? The answers to these questions and others are found in Numbers 27:12–23. Also revealed in this ancient record are maxims that will help us when we seek new leaders and/or turn our positions over to others to fill.

I. A Review of Some Essential Information.
It is important for us to recall God's reason for not permitting Moses to enter Canaan—he had publicly tarnished the Lord's glory in a fit of rage (Num. 20:7–13). This left a void in leadership that had to be filled. But who was qualified to replace Moses? There were only two available candidates—Caleb and Joshua. Among those who had been a part of the Exodus, they were the only ones God would allow to enter the Promised Land (Num. 14:30). And of these two men, only Joshua had been "the attendant of Moses from his youth" (Num. 11:28). That is, Moses had been personally training Joshua to take a leadership role. Because of this, Joshua was the most qualified candidate.

II. The Appointment of Moses' Successor.
As we probe into the events surrounding the selection and initiation of Moses' replacement, let's bear in mind this central principle: *When a man of God dies, nothing of God dies.* The Lord's chosen individual for a particular position will eventually pass on. But God's work in people's lives will continue to flourish. This truth is definitely borne out in the removal of Moses and the installation of Joshua. Let's see how this important transition was made.

    A. Viewing the Land. After keeping them for forty years in the barren desert, God finally led the Israelites to the border of Canaan. Following their arrival, the Lord said to Moses, " 'Go up to this mountain of Abarim, and see the land which I have given to the sons of Israel. And when you have seen it, you too shall be gathered to your people, as Aaron your brother was; for in the wilderness of Zin,...you rebelled against My command to treat Me as holy before their eyes at the water' " (Num. 27:12–14a). God desired to give Moses an opportunity to see the Promised Land so that he would realize that the Lord keeps His word. However, because of his disobedience at Meribah, Moses would have to die before the Hebrews crossed the Canaanite border.

B. Choosing the Man. The fact that Moses could not enter the land did not fill him with self-pity. Indeed, his greatest concern was for the Hebrews, not himself. Realizing their need for a qualified man to lead them into Canaan, Moses requested that the Lord who knows " 'the spirits of all flesh' " would " 'appoint a man over the congregation.' " He asked for a man who would lead them like a shepherd (vv. 15–17; cf. 1 Sam. 16:6–7). Moses did not try to select his successor; rather, he elected to make God's choice his own. And the Lord did not disappoint him. Without hesitation, "the Lord said to Moses, 'Take Joshua the son of Nun, a man in whom is the Spirit, and lay your hand on him; and have him stand before Eleazar the priest and before all the congregation; and commission him in their sight' " (Num. 27:18–19). By laying his hand on Joshua, Moses would be conferring his authority on him. This act would declare to the Israelites that Joshua held the reigns of leadership and therefore was to be obeyed (v. 20).

C. Following the Plan. "Moses did just as the Lord commanded him; and he took Joshua and set him before Eleazar the priest, and before all the congregation. Then he laid his hands on him and commissioned him, just as the Lord had spoken through Moses" (vv. 22–23). Moses harbored no bitterness. Once he knew who God had chosen to replace him, he took the necessary steps to see God's man officially and publicly placed into service.

III. Some Principles of Biblical Procedure.

This straightforward account of a crucial transition in Israel's leadership conveys three truths that we would be wise to accept and apply.

A. When God removes, He replaces. The Lord never runs out of potential servants. What we should do is pray that we will be sensitive enough to recognize His replacements.

B. When God appoints, He approves. As the Lord's chosen leaders take control, they will find themselves and their work blessed by God. When we find ourselves under such people, we need to pray and work for their success.

C. When God sustains, He gives success. As long as the people God selects for a position submit to His control in their lives, their work will never be characterized by failure. We can help promote and maintain the success of God's leaders and ministries by praying for them, giving to them, and cooperating with them.

☙ Living Insights

Leadership is like a relay race—it's often won or lost in the passing of the baton. We've studied the transition from Moses to Joshua. Now let's observe another historic "baton pass."

- Turn to 1 Kings 1–2. In these ninety-nine verses, Solomon takes over the throne of his father, David. As you read this passage, jot down the principles you find on filling the shoes of a leader. Use a copy of the chart below to help you organize your thoughts.

Principles on Filling a Leader's Shoes—1 Kings 1–2	
Verses	Principles

![Living Insights logo] **Living Insights**

Our study concluded with some principles of biblical procedure. Have you seen God remove, appoint, or sustain Christian leaders? Have you ever been a recipient of God's activity in the area of leadership? Make a copy of the following charts. Then write out some of your observations on how God has fulfilled these principles in your life or someone else's. After you have done this, you may want to take extra time to pray for these truths to become reality in the lives of some leaders you know.

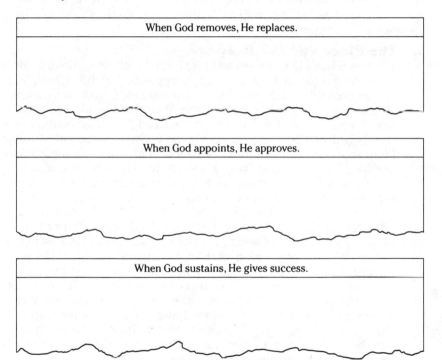

When God removes, He replaces.

When God appoints, He approves.

When God sustains, He gives success.

Obituary of a Hero
Deuteronomy 34

When you die, what would you like people to remember about you? If it was left up to others to compose the inscription on your tombstone, what do you think they would write? These are tough questions to answer because they force us to reflect seriously on our lives and to deal honestly with our goals and priorities. Unfortunately, too few of us will face these issues before we die. In this lesson we hope to thwart our tendency to ignore these significant questions. For here we will have the opportunity to meditate on our lives as we consider Moses' death. The benefits will be great, but they cannot be received unless we become vulnerable to the message in Deuteronomy 34—Moses' obituary.

I. The Place and the Purpose.
The text tells us that "Moses went up from the plains of Moab to Mount Nebo, to the top of Pisgah, which is opposite Jericho" (Deut. 34:1a). *Pisgah* probably refers to a ridge that extended from the summit of Mount Nebo.* Nebo is a part of the Abarim mountain range, which lies just east of what is now called the Dead Sea. This mountain rises to a height of 4,500 feet, making it the highest in the entire range.†
From this vantage point, the Lord showed Moses all of the Promised Land— "Gilead as far as Dan, and all Naphtali and the land of Ephraim and Manasseh, and all the land of Judah as far as the western sea, and the Negev and the plain in the valley of Jericho, the city of palm trees, as far as Zoar" (vv. 1b–3). Again the Lord fulfilled His word to Moses (cf. Deut. 32:48–52). Although he was not allowed to enter the land, he was given the joy of seeing the riches that the Hebrews were going to inherit (Deut. 34:4). Soon after he completed his survey, "Moses the servant of the Lord died . . . in the land of Moab, according to the word of the Lord" (v. 5). There are two facts we should notice in this account of his death. First, *he died alone.* There were no family members or friends at his side when he passed away. This does not imply that Moses went to his grave lonely—longing in vain to reach out to somebody. Rather, it means that he departed without farewells or fanfare. Second, *he died secure.* There was no question that Moses was God's servant. He died forever safe in the loving arms of the Lord. And he passed on in accordance with God's timetable. Moses' days were over, so God took his life.

---

*Jack S. Deere, "Deuteronomy," in *The Bible Knowledge Commentary,* edited by John F. Walvoord and Roy B. Zuck (Wheaton: Victor Books, 1985), p. 322.

†James E. Jennings, "Nebo," in *The New International Dictionary of Biblical Archaeology,* edited by Edward M. Blaiklock and R. K. Harrison (Grand Rapids: Regency Reference Library, Zondervan Publishing House, 1983), p. 331.

II. The Report and the Record.

In recounting Moses' death, the biblical text communicates various pieces of information that give us a good deal of insight into this man.

A. His Age. The account informs us that "Moses was one hundred and twenty years old when he died" (v. 7a). Reflecting on his life, Moses must have marveled at how much he had experienced and matured. He had come a long way since the time the Lord had spared his young life with a wicker basket strategically placed in the Nile River.

B. His Condition. Although Moses died at the age of one hundred and twenty, he was in remarkable physical condition. Indeed, "his eye was not dim, nor his vigor abated" (v. 7b). Another indication of his excellent health was his hike up Mount Nebo. For it must have taken a strong person to be able to climb a mountain that was almost a mile high ... especially after he had spent forty years leading the Hebrews through desolate deserts. Obviously, Moses did not allow himself to *grow old,* sitting on the sidelines watching life pass by. Instead, he *matured with grace.* He chose to deepen his relationship with God and strengthen his service to people. As a consequence, he died in top spiritual condition. We are told that since his departure, "no prophet has risen in Israel like Moses, whom the Lord knew face to face" (v. 10). Other prophets came who knew of the Lord and received revelations from Him, but they could not have had inscribed on their tombstones, "I had an altogether unique relationship with the living God." Only Moses could make such a claim.

C. His Memory. Although the Hebrew people had bickered with Moses often, they continued to feel a deep love for him. After all, he constantly manifested his devotion to them by serving them unselfishly in the Exodus and during their wanderings in the wilderness. So when he died, they "wept for Moses in the plains of Moab thirty days"—a long time to grieve over the loss of a leader (v. 8a). But once the month had ended, they stopped weeping even though they never ceased remembering (v. 8b). The people would never forget "all the mighty power and ... all the great terror which Moses [as God's instrument] performed in the sight of all Israel" (v. 12).

III. The Life and the Lessons.

Certainly, Moses was a colossal figure in human history, but this does not mean that we cannot achieve what he attained. In fact, this closing record of his death teaches us at least three truths that we can all apply to our lives.

A. The secret of fulfillment in life is involvement. Moses never retired from serving people or learning God's Word. He stayed in touch with those things that are everlasting. This gave his life length. Do you want a fulfilling life? Get involved; don't withdraw.

B. The secret of reality in life is humility. Moses never became enthralled with his own track record. His humility made him believable and vulnerable to others. This gave his life breadth. Do you want a real life? Seek to exalt others, not yourself.

C. The secret of happiness in life is perspective. Although Moses faced many situations that could have brought on feelings of despair, he rarely fell prey to those traps. Instead, he turned to the Lord and drew his strength and answers from His unlimited resources. This approach gave his life depth. Do you want a happy life? Look at life from God's perspective. And give your burdens to Him; don't carry them yourself.

🐾 *Living Insights*

Study One ▬▬▬▬▬▬▬▬▬▬▬▬▬▬▬▬▬▬▬▬▬▬▬▬▬▬

God doesn't let us see Moses' grave site, but He does allow us to read the tombstone. Let's continue to develop the theme of this lesson— "Obituary of a Hero."

- Carefully reread Deuteronomy 34. Write an obituary of Moses, using this chapter as a springboard. Feel free to go back into the previous studies to fill in more details on the life of this great hero. Be sure to include both his strengths and his weaknesses. This exercise will serve as a good vehicle for *review,* which we'll do even more thoroughly in our final lesson.

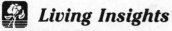 *Living Insights*

Study Two ━━━━━━━━━━━━━━━━━━━━━━━━━━━━

We seldom think about how our own tombstone or obituary will read. But since this study speaks so directly to that issue, it would be wise to conclude with some personal reflection.

- How do you want to be remembered? What words would you like to appear on your tombstone? What descriptive phrases would you hope to see in your obituary? Obviously, these questions simply serve as means to help us examine our goals and priorities. Are you now living in a way that will cultivate those qualities by which you want to be remembered? If not, then let your answers to these questions reveal some areas in your life that need to be changed. Then take some specific steps toward making those changes.

Moses' Faith,
Moses' Choices . . . and Me
Hebrews 11:24–28

As we have seen from our study, Moses made choices that were anything but simple and painless. But even though they were difficult, the decisions he made were vital to his relationship with God and the Lord's people. It's true that he committed some errors along the way. However, the life he modeled is one characterized by great faith. Because of this truth, it would be good for us to take one last look at Moses' life—especially at those choices that marked him as a faithful man of God. These critical decisions have been succinctly preserved for us in Hebrews 11:24–28. So let's take some time to concentrate on this passage in order to see how we may improve our walk with God.

I. Moses' Life in Review.
Moses was a great man in many ways. While growing up in Egypt, he became eloquent in speech and influential in achievements. He was also God's chosen instrument for humbling Pharaoh and leading the Hebrews out of Egypt. In addition, he guided and served the Israelites for forty years in the wilderness and brought them to the border of the Promised Land. Of course, Moses had weaknesses. But when we consider what he gave up in order to walk by faith, we can appreciate his life even more fully. After all, he grew up in the wealthy land of Egypt and was raised in the palace of the king. Consequently, he enjoyed all the comforts, benefits, and honors of royalty. Great treasures and political prowess were within his reach. And yet, he exchanged it all for something better—a life of trust in the living God.

II. Moses' Faith in Operation.
The life Moses chose to lead did not bring him any recognition in Egypt. We would look in vain for a sphinx, pyramid, or statue erected in his honor. Why didn't the Egyptians acknowledge his greatness? Because he made three significant decisions that separated him from his Egyptian peers. Let's briefly examine each one.

A. He refused to sustain the sinful.
The writer of Hebrews conveyed this fact in these words: "By faith Moses, when he had grown up, *refused* to be called the son of Pharaoh's daughter; *choosing* rather to endure ill-treatment with the people of God, than to enjoy the passing pleasures of sin; *considering* the reproach of Christ greater riches than the treasures of Egypt; for he was looking to the reward" (Heb. 11:24–26, emphasis added). Moses did not make this decision in haste. He undoubtedly knew the serious repercussions such a choice would have. But he had to decide between embracing the temporal at the expense of the

102

eternal or shunning the temporal for the rewards of the eternal. By faith, Moses chose to walk the path of God. In so doing, he refused to adopt the career his Egyptian contemporaries expected him to pursue. Moses' decision consisted of two ingredients: a choice to endure suffering rather than enjoy sin, and a focus on the everlasting reward in Christ rather than on the perishing riches in Egypt. Although his faith in the Lord led him to be forgotten in Egypt, it did not lead to obscurity in God's sight. The Lord esteemed him on earth, and He will exalt him in heaven.

B. He determined to leave the familiar. "By faith," we are told, Moses "left Egypt, not fearing the wrath of the king; for he endured, as seeing Him who is unseen" (v. 27). Moses' attention was riveted on the living God rather than on the Egyptian king. This gave him the courage to confront Pharaoh and leave for Canaan—a land that he had never seen. Moses chose to venture rather than vegetate, to risk rather than rust.

C. He was willing to do the unusual. By faith, Moses did what had never been done before. For example, "he kept the Passover"—an ordinance that involved sprinkling the blood of a lamb on the doorway and lintel of one's home (Exod. 12:1–28). Why? So that the death angel would not enter and kill the firstborn within (Heb. 11:28). Moses was also God's instrument for parting the Red Sea and leading the Israelites safely through it (v. 29). Nothing similar to these events had ever occurred in human history. And yet, without any tradition to fall back on, Moses was willing to obey God even at the expense of being ridiculed or misunderstood.

III. Our Choices Today.

We dare not exalt Moses above the level of humanity. But neither should we ignore what can be learned from his life. From our study in Hebrews 11, three truths emerge regarding Moses' behavior. They are principles that we should all apply to our lives.

A. To have the discernment it takes to refuse the sinful, faith must overshadow our feelings. What do you need to refuse?

B. To have the determination it takes to leave the familiar, faith must be our security. What do you need to leave?

C. To have the discipline it takes to do the unusual, faith must silence our critics. What do you need to accomplish?

🐝 *Living Insights*

With this final lesson, we bring to a close the study of a great man. We've gone from the reeds by the bank of the Nile to the top of Mount Nebo . . . from a three-month-old baby in a basket to a one-hundred-and-twenty-year-old man in a grave. Let's wrap up this study with a *review*.

- Copy the following chart into your notebook. Then flip back through the pages of your Bible, study guide, and notebook, concentrating on the first ten lessons. As you retrace your steps, look for one special truth and one important application from each study, then write them down in the appropriate column.

Moses: God's Man for a Crisis		
Lesson Titles	Special Truths	Important Applications
Misery, Midwives, and Murder		
Born After Midnight		
God's Will, My Way		
Lessons Learned from Failure		
The Desert: School of Self-discovery		
Burning Bridges or Burning Bushes		
Who Me, Lord?		
God's Will, God's Way		
Going from Bad to Worse		
Plagues That Preach		

104

⚜ *Living Insights*

Let's continue our review of the life of Moses by zeroing in on the last ten lessons.

* After you copy the following chart into your notebook, resume your review with the lessons listed below. And remember, you're looking for a special truth and an important application from each study.

Moses: God's Man for a Crisis		
Lesson Titles	Special Truths	Important Applications
The Night Nobody Slept		
Between the Devil and the Deep Red Sea		
A Heavenly Diet vs. an Earthly Appetite		
Why Leaders Crack Up		
Sinai: Where Moses Met God		
Particular Perils of the Godly		
A Moment of Rage		
Filling the Shoes of Moses		
Obituary of a Hero		
Moses' Faith, Moses' Choices . . . and Me		

Books for Probing Further

Our study of Moses has touched on a number of subjects. For instance, our knowledge of God was deepened as we learned about His most intimate name—*YHWH.* We gained a greater appreciation of worship when we witnessed the Israelites preparing for their meeting with God at Mount Sinai. Furthermore, we discerned some practical principles on leading people and handling emotions while we watched how Moses dealt with the Hebrews in the wilderness. Also, from Moses' desert experiences in Midian, we unearthed some guidelines on discovering God's will and learned some lessons on gaining from failure. We even realized afresh the need to understand Scripture as we saw Israel worship God and how to deal with death as we read Moses' obituary. Because so many subjects have been covered in this study, we have elected to provide you with a list of some of the best resources on eight of these topics. Our desire is that you use the books given below as supplements—not as substitutes—to Bible study and Christian living.

I. Knowing God.

Bavinck, Herman. *The Doctrine of God.* Translated, edited, and outlined by William Hendriksen. Grand Rapids: Baker Book House, 1977.

Baxter, J. Sidlow. *Majesty: The God You Should Know.* San Bernardino: Here's Life Publishers, 1984.

Charnock, Stephen. *The Existence and Attributes of God.* 2 vols. Grand Rapids: Baker Book House, 1979.

France, R. T. *The Living God.* Downers Grove: InterVarsity Press, 1970.

Hocking, David L. *The Nature of God in Plain Language.* Waco: Word Books, 1984.

Lewis, C. S. *Mere Christianity.* Rev. ed. New York: Macmillan Publishing Co., Inc., 1952.

Nystrom, Carolyn. *Who Is God?* Illustrated by Wayne A. Hanna. Children's Bible Basics. Chicago: Moody Press, 1980.

Packer, J. I. *Knowing God.* Downers Grove: InterVarsity Press, 1973.

Shedd, William G. T. *Dogmatic Theology.* Vol. 1. Reprint. Minneapolis: Klock & Klock Christian Publishers, 1979.

Strauss, Richard L. *The Joy of Knowing God.* Neptune: Loizeaux Brothers, Inc., 1984.

Thiessen, Henry Clarence. *Lectures in Systematic Theology.* Revised by Vernon D. Doerksen. Grand Rapids: William B. Eerdmans Publishing Co., 1979.

Tozer, A. W. *The Knowledge of the Holy.* San Francisco: Harper and Row, 1961.

II. Worshiping God.

Allen, Ronald, and Borror, Gordon. *Worship: Rediscovering the Missing Jewel.* A Critical Concern Book. Portland: Multnomah Press, 1982.

Eastman, Dick. *A Celebration of Praise: Exciting Prospects for Extraordinary Praise.* Grand Rapids: Baker Book House, 1984.

Howard, Thomas. *Evangelical Is Not Enough.* Nashville: Thomas Nelson Publishers, 1984.

Martin, Ralph P. *Worship in the Early Church.* Reprint. Grand Rapids: William B. Eerdmans Publishing Co., 1978.

Schaper, Robert N. *In His Presence: Appreciating Your Worship Tradition.* Nashville: Thomas Nelson Publishers, 1984.

Webber, Robert E. *Worship Is a Verb.* Waco: Word Books, 1985.

Webber, Robert E. *Worship Old and New.* Ministry Resources Library. Grand Rapids: Zondervan Publishing House, 1982.

III. Discovering God's Will.

Friesen, Garry. *Decision Making and the Will of God: A Biblical Alternative to the Traditional View.* With J. Robin Maxson. A Critical Concern Book. Portland: Multnomah Press, 1980.

Friesen, Garry, and Maxson, J. Robin. *Principles for Decision Making: Living according to God's Will.* Portland: Multnomah Press, 1984.

MacArthur, John, Jr. *Found: God's Will.* Wheaton: Victor Books, 1973.

Sproul, R. C. *God's Will and the Christian.* Wheaton: Tyndale House Publishers, 1984.

Swindoll, Charles R. *God's Will: Biblical Direction for Living.* Portland: Multnomah Press, 1981.

Willard, Dallas. *In Search of Guidance: Developing a Conversational Relationship with God.* Ventura: Regal Books, 1984.

Yancey, Philip. *Guidance: Making Sense of God's Directions.* Portland: Multnomah Press, 1983.

IV. Understanding Scripture.

Archer, Gleason L. *Encyclopedia of Bible Difficulties.* Foreword by Kenneth S. Kantzer. Grand Rapids: Zondervan Publishing House, 1982.

Barber, Cyril J. *Dynamic Personal Bible Study.* Foreword by Charles C. Ryrie. Neptune: Loizeaux Brothers, 1981.

Berkhof, L. *Principles of Biblical Interpretation.* Grand Rapids: Baker Book House, 1950.

Blanchard, John. *How to Enjoy Your Bible.* Welwyn: Evangelical Press, 1984.

Ellisen, Stanley A. *Knowing God's Word.* Nashville: Thomas Nelson Publishers, 1984.

Haley, John W. *Alleged Discrepancies of the Bible.* Introduction by Alvah Hovey. Reprint. Grand Rapids: Baker Book House, 1977.

Henrichsen, Walter A. *A Layman's Guide to Interpreting the Bible.* Rev. and exp. ed. Grand Rapids: Zondervan Publishing House; Colorado Springs: NavPress, 1978.

Herr, Ethel L. *Bible Study for Busy Women.* Chicago: Moody Press, 1982.

Jenkins, Simon. *Bible Mapbook.* Belleville: Lion Publishing, 1985.
May, Herbert G., ed. *Oxford Bible Atlas.* 2d ed. London: Oxford University Press, 1974.
Millard, Alan. *Treasures from Bible Times.* Belleville: Lion Publishing, 1985.
Packer, J. I.; Tenney, Merrill C.; and White, William, Jr., eds. *The Bible Almanac.* Nashville: Thomas Nelson Publishers, 1980.
Sterrett, T. Norton. *How to Understand Your Bible.* Rev. ed. Downers Grove: InterVarsity Press, 1974.
Stott, John R. W. *Understanding the Bible.* Reprint. Glendale: Regal Books, 1973.
Unger, Merrill F. *Unger's Bible Dictionary.* 3d ed., rev. Chicago: Moody Press, 1966.
Vos, Howard F. *Effective Bible Study: A Guide to Sixteen Methods.* Grand Rapids: Zondervan Publishing House, 1956.
Wald, Oletta. *The Joy of Discovery in Bible Study.* Rev. ed. Minneapolis: Augsburg Publishing House, 1975.

V. Leading People.

Anderson, Robert C. *The Effective Pastor.* Chicago: Moody Press, 1985.
Baker, Don. *Leadership: Learning to Make Others Succeed.* Portland: Multnomah Press, 1983.
Barber, Cyril J. *Nehemiah and the Dynamics of Effective Leadership.* Neptune: Loizeaux Brothers, 1976.
Barber, Cyril J., and Strauss, Gary H. *Leadership: The Dynamics of Success.* Foreword by Dr. Vernon C. Grounds. Greenwood: The Attic Press, 1982.
Bratchard, Edward B. *The Walk-on-Water Syndrome.* Foreword by Wayne Oates. Waco: Word Books, 1984.
Campbell, Donald K. *Nehemiah: Man in Charge.* Wheaton: Victor Books, 1979.
Eims, LeRoy. *Be a Motivational Leader.* Foreword by Charles R. Swindoll. Wheaton: Victor Books, 1981.
Eims, LeRoy. *Be the Leader You Were Meant to Be.* Foreword by Theodore H. Epp. Wheaton: Victor Books, 1975.
Hocking, David L. *Be a Leader People Follow.* Ventura: Regal Books, 1979.
Peterson, Eugene H. *Five Smooth Stones for Pastoral Work.* Atlanta: John Knox Press, 1980.
Sanders, J. Oswald. *Paul the Leader.* Colorado Springs: NavPress, 1984.
Stott, John R. W. *The Preacher's Portrait: Some New Testament Word Studies.* Grand Rapids: William B. Eerdmans Publishing Co., 1961.
Sugden, Howard F., and Wiersbe, Warren W. *Confident Pastoral Leadership.* Chicago: Moody Press, 1973.

Swindoll, Charles R. *Hand Me Another Brick*. Nashville: Thomas Nelson Publishers, 1978.

Swindoll, Chuck. *Leadership*. Lifemaps series. Waco: Word Books, 1985.

VI. Learning from Failure.

Lutzer, Erwin W. *Failure: The Back Door to Success*. Chicago: Moody Press, 1984.

Lutzer, Erwin W. *When a Good Man Falls*. Wheaton: Victor Books, 1985.

Mehl, Duane. *At Peace with Failure*. Minneapolis: Augsburg Publishing House, 1984.

Merrill, Dean. *Another Chance: How God Overrides Our Big Mistakes*. Grand Rapids: Zondervan Publishing House, 1981.

Swindoll, Charles R. *Encourage Me*. Portland: Multnomah Press, 1982.

Swindoll, Charles R. *Starting Over: Fresh Hope for the Road Ahead*. Portland: Multnomah Press, 1977.

Weese, Wightman. *Back in Touch*. Wheaton: Tyndale House Publishers, Inc., 1984.

VII. Handling Emotions.

Albin, Rochelle Semmel. *Emotions*. Choices series. Philadelphia: The Westminster Press, 1983.

Baker, Don, and Nester, Emery. *Depression: Finding Hope and Meaning in Life's Darkest Shadow*. A Critical Concern Book. Portland: Multnomah Press, 1983.

Carter, Les. *Mind Over Emotions: How to Mentally Control Your Feelings*. Grand Rapids: Baker Book House, 1985.

Dobson, James, Dr. *Emotions: Can You Trust Them?* Ventura: Regal Books, 1980.

Lutzer, Erwin. *Managing Your Emotions*. Wheaton: Victor Books, 1983.

Miller, Kathy Collard. *When Love Becomes Anger*. San Bernardino: Here's Life Publishers, 1985.

Neff, Miriam. *Women and Their Emotions*. Chicago: Moody Press, 1984.

Reeve, Pamela. *Overcome Your Worry: Handling Fear and Anxiety*. Portland: Multnomah Press, 1984.

Sell, Charles M. *Getting through Depression: A Path to Hope and Healing*. Portland: Multnomah Press, 1984.

Swindoll, Charles R. *Anger: The Burning Fuse of Hostility*. Portland: Multnomah Press, 1980.

Walters, Richard P. *Anger: Yours and Mine and What to Do about It*. Grand Rapids: Zondervan Publishing House, 1981.

Warren, Neil Clark. *Make Anger Your Ally: Harnessing Our Most Baffling Emotion*. Garden City: A Doubleday-Galilee Book, 1985.

VIII. Dealing with Death.

Anderson, J. Kerby. *Life, Death, and Beyond*. Grand Rapids: Zondervan Publishing House, 1980.

Attlee, Rosemary. *William's Story: A Mother's Account of Her Son's Struggle against Cancer.* Wheaton: Harold Shaw Publishers, 1983.

Bayly, Joseph. *The Last Thing We Talk About.* Rev. ed. Elgin: David C. Cook Publishing Co., 1973.

Dobihal, Edward F., Jr., and Stewart, Charles William. *When a Friend Is Dying: A Guide to Caring for the Terminally Ill and Bereaved.* Nashville: Abingdon Press, 1984.

Ford, Leighton. *Sandy: A Heart for God.* Downers Grove: InterVarsity Press, 1985.

Kreeft, Peter J. *Love Is Stronger Than Death.* San Francisco: Harper and Row, 1979.

Lewis, C. S. *A Grief Observed.* New York: The Seabury Press, 1961.

Manning, Doug. *Comforting Those Who Grieve: A Guide for Helping Others.* San Francisco: Harper and Row, 1985.

Manning, Doug. *Don't Take My Grief Away: What to Do When You Lose a Loved One.* Reprint. San Francisco: Harper and Row, 1984.

Means, James E. *A Tearful Celebration.* Portland: Multnomah Press, 1985.

Morey, Robert A., Dr. *Death and the Afterlife.* Foreword by Walter Martin. Minneapolis: Bethany House Publishers, 1984.

Nystrom, Carolyn. *What Happens When We Die?* Illustrated by Wayne A. Hanna. Children's Bible Basics. Chicago: Moody Press, 1981.

Richards, Larry, and Johnson, Paul, M.D. *Death and the Caring Community: Ministering to the Terminally Ill.* A Critical Concern Book. Portland: Multnomah Press, 1980.

Richardson, Jean. *A Death in the Family.* Belleville: Lion Publishing Corporation, 1985.

Sell, Charles M. *Grief's Healing Process: Understanding and Accepting Your Loss.* Portland: Multnomah Press, 1984.

Sherrill, John. *Mother's Song.* Grand Rapids: Chosen Books, The Zondervan Corporation, 1982.

Vredevelt, Pam W. *Empty Arms: Emotional Support for Those Who Have Suffered Miscarriage and Stillbirth.* Portland: Multnomah Press, 1984.